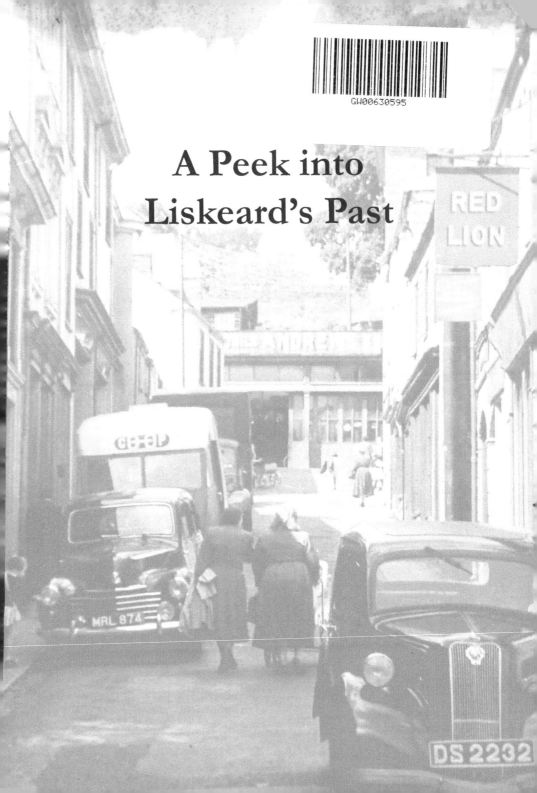

A Peek into Liskeard's Past

First published 2022

Liskeard & District Museum www.liskeardmuseum.com

ISBN: 978 1 3999 1260 0

Printed in Padstow by TJ Books

PREFACE

John Allen's *'History of the Borough of Liskeard and its Vicinity'* written in 1856 is a thorough and valuable resource for those of us who are keen to learn of the Charters, Mayoral Records and Manuscripts dating back to the year 1000 when our town was first documented, in relation to the manumission of a female slave in Lyscerruyt. As interesting as Allen's book is, I have adopted an entirely different approach, to avoid repetition and, hopefully, to give you something new and interesting to read about. My approach has been to take a *'small snippet'* of information and develop it further using family history sites, censuses, trade directories, newspaper reports etc. The source of the original *'snippets'* are various; the cemetery headstone that gives the cause of death *'by the falling of a block of granite while he superintended the erection of the Town Hall'*. Or the newspaper report concerning an elderly gentleman in the early days of motoring walking in the middle of the road, which put a car driver *'in a quandary'* as to how to avoid him (the car hit a granite stone and a passenger was thrown out on to the street!).

I have purposely avoided concentrating on the well to-do Victorian Gentlemen, of which there were many in Liskeard in the 19th and early 20th centuries, as I felt it would give the false impression that life was wonderful for one and all. So as well as the occasional Attorney and Mayor, I've written about the pauper in the workhouse, the children working in the mines and living in squalor and the shopkeepers, of which there were many in the busy market town of Liskeard.

My grateful thanks go to Liskeard & District Museum and Liskeard Old Cornwall Society for access to their archives and their permission to reproduce the images you will see in this book. These archive rooms are open, free of charge, to the public for reading and research. Also my thanks go to Gwyneth McLoughlin for her advice in the very beginning with grammar and punctuation, to Jo Hoskin for guiding me through the fascinating art of Graphic Design, and to Pauline Hubner for her valuable input in the latter stages of the project. It's pleasing to note that all three ladies, and myself, are resident in Liskeard making this a truly 'local' production.

As much as I enjoy researching the people and places of the town to which I have become attached, the real pleasure is from sharing the results with others, hence this publication, so I hope you enjoy the reading as much as I have enjoyed the writing.

Brian Oldham
Liskeard
January 2022

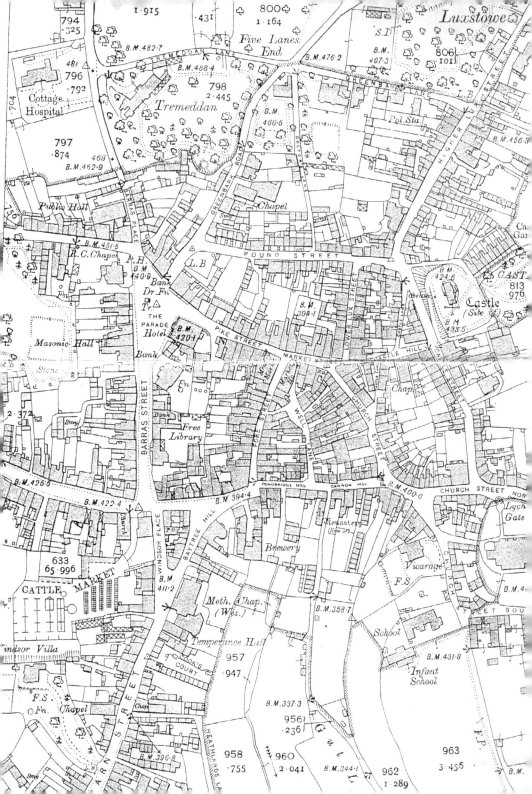

FOREWORD

As Mayor of Liskeard, I am all too aware of the contribution Brian Oldham has, and continues to have, in preserving and bringing the history of our town, and of Cornwall to the present.

Brian Oldham is without a doubt our town's unofficial, Official Historian. As a volunteer at Liskeard & District Museum, and as President of the Liskeard Old Cornwall Society, Brian can often be found researching the history of people's homes or answering questions from residents on social media about their past. His research work in our museum has led to a huge font of knowledge appertaining to all things Liskeard; he manages to bring our town's history alive like no other. He is the go-to person on all things historical in Liskeard and the wider area.

He does this by concentrating not on the great and the good, but by telling the story of the everyday residents of Liskeard. He makes history personal and brings to life those all too often forgotten in today's history books. From History Walks around our town – where he often says "look up and see what everyone misses" to leading tours of our Mining Heritage, and even appearing on the television, his wealth of knowledge is unprecedented.

His promotion of the Cornish Identity, its traditions and its history, are a testament to his passion for Cornwall. Bringing old traditions to life and ensuring their continued existence is paramount to Brian.

As you will see as you read on, this book is well researched, funny in parts, sad in others, but ultimately brings Liskeard alive and tells the story of some of its forgotten inhabitants and their daily lives, from Cricketing Vicars to the Married Widows of Addington.

Cllr Simon Cassidy
His Worship the Mayor of Liskeard
January 2022

Liskeard Town Centre Map 1905

DESERTED IN THE WORKHOUSE
THE DAVEY FAMILY

Jessie was born in 1859 in Rilla Mill, the second youngest of the ten children of copper miner John Carkeet and his wife Julia. At least three of her brothers were also copper miners. She married Tin Miner William John Davey in 1877 when they were 18 and 17 years old respectively. They settled in the Liverscombe area of Rilla Mill and by the 1881 census had two daughters: Charlotte (3) and Harriet (10 months).

Big changes had occurred by 1891 when Jessie Davey (32) was an inmate in the Liskeard Union Workhouse in Station Road with four of her children: Harriet (11), James (9), Lilly (6) and Charles (5). Jessie's situation is given as '*Able Bodied, Wife of Copper Miner (deserted)*'. In her book *The Married Widows of Cornwall*, Lesley Trotter describes Jessie as '*the only explicit reference in any Cornish census returns to a miner's wife in extreme poverty*'.

It is very likely that the errant husband and father, William John Davey, was part of the great Cornish Diaspora, as there is no record of him in England after the 1881 census. However, in the 1900 census for Suffolk County, Massachusetts, there appears a William Davey born in England in June 1860. Cornish Diaspora is the term given to the mass emigration of miners during the 19th century when the low price of tin and copper, and competition from abroad, led to the closure of many mines in Cornwall.

Rilla Mill village with Liverscombe top centre

Liskeard Union Workhouse, Station Road in the 1930s which was opened in 1839 to house 350 in-mates.

They sought employment in many destinations across the world, but particularly North and South America, South Africa and Australia.

When her siblings were in the Union Workhouse, eldest daughter Charlotte, at 13, was a scholar at the Deaf and Dumb Institution in Topsham Road, Exeter, along with forty-three other children, twenty-six boys and seventeen girls, aged between 7 and 15. There were nine staff living-in in 1891 and Charlotte was registered as Deaf and Dumb.

The family had all gone their separate ways by 1901, but hopefully kept in touch with each other. Jessie (42) was widowed and employed as a Cook for the eighty-three inmates of the Clarence Place Workhouse in Plymouth. Charlotte (23) was in Service with the family of Post Office Superintendent Benjamin Gribbell, in Plymouth. Harriet (20) was Cook for the Trood family in Spriddlestone House, Brixton St Mary. James (18) was an Ordinary Seaman on HMS Illustrious, a battleship stationed in Malta (James later rose to Petty Officer 1st Class on HMS Skipjack). Lilly (16) was in Service with the family of the Tamar Manure Works Manager John Abbott in Gunnislake. Charles (15) was an Apprentice Chair Maker in Yealmpton.

HE MANIPULATED EVERYTHING
CHARLES ALFRED MILLMAN AND LISKEARD'S PASSIVE RESISTERS

On May 8th 1899 William Nicholas Connock Marshall, Gentleman of Treworgey, leased a close of land in Station Road known as Tollgate Meadow to Joseph Sweet, stonemason, Richard Hawkey Runnalls, carpenter and John Sparks Elliott, carpenter, all of Liskeard. The term was ninety nine years with rent of £6 per year, but within twelve months at least £1500 had to be spent on building seven good and substantial dwelling houses. They were named Victoria Terrace.

Joseph Sweet, who in 1901 gave his occupation as 'Stonemason and Fruiterer', occupied No.7 until October 16th 1907 when he transferred the remaining ninety one years of his lease to Charles Alfred Millman, Political Agent of Liskeard. A deposit of £500 was paid plus a yearly rent of 12s 6d. Millman's widow Elizabeth Priscilla bought the freehold from the Squire of Treworgey twenty seven years later for £25.

Charles (46) and Elizabeth (36) are listed in the 1911 census at No.7 with their son Alfred Garfield (13) and their domestic servant, 18 year old Bessie Riddle from Quethiock. Charles' occupation was given as Liberal Registration Agent.

Victoria Terrace, Liskeard

No.7 Victoria Terrace, Station Road is the end house on the right

On March 27th 1905 three leading Liskeard Methodists were sentenced to seven days imprisonment, for non-payment of the Education Rate, by the Liskeard Magistrates. Mr. R.M. Botterell, Rev. R. Squire and Mr. C.A. Millman were dubbed '*Liskeard's Passive Resisters*'. Their argument was that their children attended private schools and they did not intend to pay twice for their education.

Millman was the Liberal Agent for 'Tommy' Agar-Robartes when the latter was elected MP for South East Cornwall on January 22nd 1906. Unfortunately, in the following June, Tommy appeared in the Bodmin Assize Court accused of '*the corrupt practices of bribery, treating and undue influence*'. Judge Grantham decided that, in the circumstances '*it was clear the seat could not be held and that Mr. Robartes should be unseated*'. The blame however, was not his nor his parents, but his agent Mr. Millman, who had '*manipulated everything*' to gain an election victory.

The Passive Resisters arriving at Liskeard Station on March 27th 1905

T.C.R. Agar-Robartes (Tommy) of Lanhydrock died during the Battle of Loos in September 1915 aged 35

The large crowd outside the Court disagreed with the verdict; Mr. Snell, the Tory agent who brought the petition, needed a police bodyguard, while Tommy Robartes and Millman were given an enthusiastic reception. On December 11th 1914 the *Cornish Times* reported that Mr. Millman had received a letter from the Secretary of State for War, Lord Kitchener, giving cordial thanks for his services in the Recruiting Drive.

Charles Alfred Millman died December 23rd 1927 aged 62 years. The inscription by Sweet & Son, whose founder had, twenty years earlier, sold No.7 Victoria Terrace to Millman, is on a granite kerb rather than a headstone in Lanchard Cemetery, Station Road.

'The prisoners were perfect strangers to him, but they had been in the neighbourhood for about a week and had been staying at the Common Lodging House'

Lodging House, Cannon Hill in the 1940s

THE CASE OF THE STOLEN BONES

WILLIAM JOHN LEE AND EMILY LEE

The Cornish Times of May 7th 1909 reported that '*Wm. John Lee and Emily Lee were charged at the Liskeard Police-court on Monday, before the Mayor (Mr. W.H. Huddy), Dr. W. Nettle and Mr. E.J. Snell, with stealing 25lbs of bones, to the value of 9d, from Mr. W.N. Crago of Trevecca Farm, Liskeard, on Saturday. Both prisoners pleaded guilty.*' William Hotten Huddy was a Watchmaker and Company Secretary of Ham & Huddy, Fore Street, Liskeard. William Nettle M.R.S.C. was a Surgeon and Medical Officer on The Parade, Liskeard. Ernest J. Snell was the proprietor of boot and shoe maker S. Snell & Son, Bay Tree Hill, Liskeard.

'*The complainant had scattered around his fields for manure a quantity of bones, which he had got from the town refuse*', but they were frequently stolen. '*On Saturday he found the prisoners in one of his fields gathering the bones; they had 1 bag full and several heaps*'. They absconded, but were apprehended at Tremar Coombe by Police Sergeant Johns and subsequently identified by Mr. Crago.

William Nicholas Crago was aged 36, unmarried and living on his father's farm at Trevecca at the time. Within two years he had his own farm at Halbathick, Liskeard, where he lived with his wife of one year, Jessie and his 2 month old daughter Mary. He had one employee, 18 year old Horace Johns whose occupation was '*Horseman on Farm*'.

Trevecca Farmhouse in 2020

Giving evidence to the Court, Police Superintendent Gard said that '*the prisoners were perfect strangers to him, but they had been in the neighbourhood for about a week and had been staying at the Common Lodging House. They had been trying to sell post-cards, for which Emily Lee had a licence for so doing*'. Both prisoners were jailed for one week, but the Pedlar's Licence was allowed to remain in force.

'TEAPOT' HAINE & FAMILY

THE HAINE FAMILY

In 1851 54 year old Butcher and Farmer Richard Haine rented a 'commodious dwelling house' in Barn Street from local landowner Samuel Trehawke Kekewich. With Richard lived his wife Mary (60), daughter Mary Ann (23) and son John (21), a Butcher with his father. To help with the family finances there were four lodgers, one was a Lead Miner and another a Cordwainer. Kekewich sold many of his properties in Liskeard at an auction held in Webb's Hotel on August 22nd 1855. One Lot was the Haine family shop and home, bought by their neighbour Betsy Chudleigh for £300. Betsy was a Baker and her son Joseph took over from the Haines' butchery.

The Haines moved to Higher Lux Street after the auction where, in 1871, Head of the Household was now Mary Ann (43) a Furniture Broker, with Richard (74) a Farmer of thirteen acres, Mary (80) Farmer's Wife and John (40) is his Father's Assistant and shown as married. Richard Haine was given the nickname *'Teapot'* when, at an auction held in the Guildhall, he successfully bid for the teapot into which the auctioneer had deposited his takings. When the auctioneer began removing his cash from the teapot Haine insisted he had bid for teapot and its contents and demanded that he be given both.

Joseph Chudleigh's Butcher Shop, Windsor Place in 1907

Higher Lux Street-home of the Haine family in 1871

Mary Ann Haine believed in the second coming of Christ and travelled to Jerusalem to meet him in 1880. She remained there until her death at the age of 87, which was reported in the West Briton on April 8th 1915. When the little money Mary Ann took with her was exhausted, she survived on contributions from her friends in Liskeard and five shillings per week from the Liskeard Patriotic Committee.

John Haine was an enumerator for the 1851 census; he was responsible for the collecting and recording the details of six hundred and two people from one hundred and seventeen households. He was complimented for making only seven small errors in all this work. In the same year John had married Amelia Oliver, a Straw Bonnet Maker from Lower Lux Street, they were both aged 30. The marriage does not appear to have been a success as, while John was living with his parents in 1871, Amelia was keeping house for her brother in Bristol and their daughter Clara Amelia Haine, aged 18 and a Linen Draper, had been living with her grandparents in Pound Lane for at least ten years. After his parents' death John boarded in a Church Street South lodging house; his occupation was Labourer and he died in 1887 aged only 56.

THE WARDROPERS OF LADYE PARK

HENRY TIMINS WARDROPER 1842 - 1912

Henry Timins Wardroper was baptised at South Hamlet, Gloucester on January 8th 1842. His mother was Laura Matilda Montague Wardroper, his father Charles performed the ceremony, it was noted that he was an Approved Minister. At age 19 Henry appears in the 1861 census as a Boarder/Pupil at Uppingham Grammar School. In 1871, at 29 and unmarried, he is lodging at Blackwellsend Green, Gloucester, and is Curate of Hartpury with a note that he has an MA from Oxford. At 39 his occupation is Clerk in Orders, Roman Catholic Priest at St. Edmunds R. C. College, Ware, in Hertfordshire.

A complete change of direction occurred in the fourth quarter of 1884 when Henry (42) married Alice Andrews (32), 10 years his junior. Alice's parents appear to have been comfortably off, living in large houses in the area around Kingsbridge, Devon. Her father, in 1881, was a retired Lieutenant Colonel on full pay employing two domestic servants. Alice's mother Julia was 15 years younger than her father Mottram Andrews.

Henry and Alice Wardroper were settled in Ladye Park near Liskeard in 1891 with two sons and two daughters. Henry was no longer a part of the Roman Catholic establishment, presumably due to his decision to marry. However, the family did attend Our Lady and St. Neot Church in West Street, Liskeard. Henry and Alice appear in the Church records several times as sponsors for Confirmations, two of their own children were confirmed there in 1903.

The four Wardroper children grew up in Ladye Park, Mary Clarice, John Baptist Francis Mary, Mary Angela and Antony Mary. Mary Clarice was born in Plymouth in the third quarter of 1885, died on August 27th 1911 aged 26 and is buried in St. Martin's Churchyard, Liskeard.

Ladye Park, near Liskeard in 2017

John Baptist Francis Mary was born on 1st Dec. 1886 in Saltash and in 1901 was a Student at Downside Abbey, Monastery and College, in Midsomer Norton, Somerset. At age 24 he was lodging in Newcastle upon Tyne, working as a Clerk to the District Auditor. In 1939 John was living at 25 Tudor Close, Sutton, Surrey with his wife Rose Marie and his unmarried sister Mary Angela, and had progressed to Assistant District Auditor. He died when living in Walberton, Arundel, Sussex on 27th September 1951 leaving in his will £169,552 in present day values.

Mary Angela was born at Ladye Park on 5th October 1888 and never married. While living with her brother John in Sutton she was Manageress of a private hotel. She died on 4th August 1963 aged 74 when living in Pinfarthing Strand, Gloucestershire. A journalist relation, John Edmond Wardroper, was Executor of her effects, present day value of £9,656. Antony Mary was born at Ladye Park in the fourth quarter of 1890 and died in the first quarter of 1913 aged 22.

Henry Timins Wardroper of Ladye Park died on May 4th 1912 at The Hydro Hotel, Sansome Walk in Worcester. Probate was granted on August 2nd to John Baptist Francis Mary Wardroper, Auditor's Clerk. Present day value of his effects was £122,000. Following the deaths of her daughter Mary Clarice in 1911, her husband Henry in 1912 and her son Antony in 1913, Alice Wardroper left Ladye Park; she's recorded as living at 3 Dean Place, Liskeard in 1919 and died in April 1933 aged 81 in Oxford.

Mary Clarice Wardroper's elaborate headstone in St. Martin's Churchyard

NUISANCES AND A NAUGHTY DOG
PARADE HOUSE

The entry for Parade House in *The Life & Works of Henry Rice* is *'This has been credited elsewhere to Rice's former employer, Robert Coad, but was very probably the work of Rice c1835 before he set up on his own. Alterations by Rice 1850'*. In his role of Inspector of Nuisances, and later Borough Surveyor, Henry Rice reported to the Corporation on the causes of cholera outbreaks in the town, usually of a sanitary nature. In 1866 he wrote of the Parade and West Street, *'The back premises in the occupation of Mr. John Sargent require immediate cleansing and draining. Likewise all the property on the South side of West Street which at present is without Drainage of any kind'*.

In the 1851 census for Parade House are John Sargent, Solicitor aged 45, his 30 year old wife Elizabeth, a daughter and three sons all of school age, and three live-in Domestic Servants. Elizabeth's 22 year old brother, Thomas Lad, who worked for Sargent as an Articled Clerk, completed the household. *The West Briton* reported on May 29th 1863 that John Sargent had opened his grounds to the *'Star of the East'* court of the Ancient Order of Foresters, to hold their annual Fete. A procession of characters from the tales of Robin Hood, including Little John and Friar Tuck, was *'witnessed by a large number of people'*. After which they enjoyed *'archery, Aunt Sally, Uncle Sam, a weighing machine and the pleasing little Maypole dancers from Plymouth, whose efficient and graceful performances highly delighted the spectators'*.

Parade House covered in ivy in the 1920s or 1930s

Duke of Cornwall Light Infantry (DCLI) volunteers assembled in 1889, Parade House is on the right.
The 1865 book 'Liskeard Nuisance Removal' can be viewed in Liskeard & District Museum

The December 14th 1872 *Cornish Times* headlined 'The Storm', '*On the Parade a large tree standing in the front of Mr. Sargent's residence was blown down, carrying the stone work of the outer wall and iron railings with it, the top branches of the tree struck the house opposite, smashing in the top windows and injuring some of the furniture in the room. It is said that two little children who had just passed by, had a very narrow escape*'.

In the Cornish Times J.K. Broad wrote in his 'While I Remember' column that a dog having bolted with a large piece of meat, the butcher hastened off to Mr. Sargent, solicitor, to know what had better be done about it. "*Of course*" said the lawyer "*the dog owner must pay. What would you consider the value of the meat?*". "*Six and six pence*" said the butcher "*and please Sir, the dog is yours*". "*Oh I see*" said Mr. Sargent "*Now in that case, my fee for advice being six shillings and eight pence, you simply hand me two pence and that puts the whole thing right*". The Sargent headstone, by the entrance to St. Martin's Church tower, confirms that John died on May 3rd 1873 aged 68, his wife Bessie, as she was known, on August 13th 1865 aged only 44 and their second son John Becket Sargent on January 3rd 1881 at just 35.

LISKEARD'S SIGNALMAN MAYOR

JACK HUBERT PITTS M. B. E., J. P.

The election of Simon Cassidy, Labour Party candidate in the recent Cornwall Council elections and employee of Great Western Railway, to become 2021 Mayor of Liskeard, is reminiscent of Jack Hubert Pitts M.B.E., J.P. (1899-1967). Jack was Liskeard's first Labour Mayor in 1937/8, 1938/9 and 1939/40 and a signalman with British Rail. Jack joined the railway company at the age of 14 and the National Union of Railwaymen at 15. In 1917, with the 48th Division Signals (R.E.), he was wounded and gassed in the 3rd Battle of Ypres and discharged as unfit for further War Service.

In September 1931 Jack was transferred from his native Wales to Liskeard and promptly joined the local Labour Party, the Royal British Legion and attended St. Martin's Church. With his wife Edith, who organised the catering for many events in the Church Hall, he lived in railway accommodation at No.3 Grove Park Cottages. They share a headstone in St. Martin's Churchyard.

The *Cornish Times* reported that '*on 7th April 1938 Liskeard's railwayman Mayor presided over a gathering of his workmates in the Stag Hotel when a presentation was made to foreman James Moon, who has retired after 44 years' service*'. Later that year the Western Morning News reported that '*Mayor Mr. J.H. Pitts, a railway signalman, was the recipient of a gold medal for 15 years' efficiency as an ambulance worker*'. 1940 saw the 700th anniversary of the granting of the first Charter to the Borough of Liskeard. Jack led the celebrations with a Church service, a Civic Luncheon at Webb's Hotel and the issue of a commemorative medal.

On June 2nd 1995, on their front page, the Cornish Times reported that one evening during 1945, Herbert Wilson, Chemist and General Manager of Burrowite Explosives at Trago Mills and Herodsfoot, and his visiting son Harold, walked to Liskeard Station from their home in Station Road, to meet Herbert's friend Jack Pitts. After working in the Civil Service with Sir William Beveridge, creator of the Welfare State, during WWII Harold Wilson intended to enter politics, but Clement Attlee told him he must first join the Labour Party. Being domicile in Liskeard through his parents, the future Prime Minister was enrolled into the Party by Jack Pitts, inside the signal-box at the end of the Liskeard Station platform.

There are two plaques in Station Road to the memory of Jack Pitts, one in appreciation of his public service and the other on a bench inscribed '*J.H. Pitts Memorial 1968 by the British Rail Staff Association*'.

Mr. J.H.Pitts J.P.
Mayor of Liskeard
1937-1940

Liskeard's clocks
were advanced by
twenty minutes in
1859 to match the
Cornwall Railway
time-table

The Jack Pitts memorial plaque
in Station Road

MINE LABOURER TO MINE CAPTAIN
HENRY HAWKEN AND HENRY PHILLIPS

In Trevilmick Cottage, close to Helman Tor, in 1841 there lived a 60 year old Tinner named Henry Hawken and his wife Jane. Being a Tinner as opposed to a Miner, Henry probably worked in the nearby Wheal Prosper Streamworks, only five hundred metres from his home. The Hawkens had two lodgers at the time, possibly relatives, Henry Phillips, a Labourer aged 13, and his 11 year old sister Catherine. Ten years later Henry and Jane Hawken were themselves lodgers, in the home of a Tin Miner at nearby Sweets House. Both gave their occupations as Pauper, Henry was registered as Blind.

Henry Phillips, however, had fared somewhat better than his former landlord. By the 1851 census he had progressed from a labourer to a Miner (Lead), most probably in one of the successful lead/silver mines in Menheniot. He was renting a small cottage at the time in Doctor's Lane, Liskeard, with his wife Ann and 1 year old daughter Annie. At an auction held in Webb's Hotel on August 22nd 1855, Henry's bid of £55 enabled him to buy the cottage he was renting, so becoming a man of property.

Cottages in Doctor's Lane

The remains of Craddock Moor Mine in 2020. Craddock Moor Mine employed 250 people in 1864, producing 1,999 tons of copper, their best year.

In their 1863 report on Caradon mines, Messrs Webb and Geach confirmed that the Mine Agent at Craddock Moor Mine was Captain Henry Phillips and the 1861 census tells us that two sons, William(6) and John(2) had arrived and the family were living in Chapel Row, Tremar. Sadly, Ann Phillips died on October 3rd 1861 aged only 33. Henry married again a few years later to Mary, twelve years his junior and they soon moved to Darite Cottage, Crow's Nest. This larger cottage was needed as by 1872 there were seven Phillips children living at home, three by first wife Ann and four by Mary.

Prompted by the closure of the mines in the Caradon area, Henry moved his family east to Tavistock where he was employed as Mine Captain with Devon Great Consols, the largest producer at that time of copper and arsenic in Europe, still employing over seven hundred people. This was the pinnacle of a career that started as a 13 year old lad labouring on the slopes of Helman Tor searching the streams for tin deposits!

Interior of the Market around 1907

The Market, Liskeard.
E 31775

FISHWIVES AND SILENT MOVIES
THE MARKET HOUSE

The first Market House at the junction of Market Street and Well Lane was built about 1574. It was a decayed and ruinous house and became the property of the town through escheat i.e. when the owner dies leaving no legal heir. In 1821/22 the old building was demolished and a new Market House was built at a cost of £800. The architect was John Foulston who charged fifteen guineas for his services. Two small shops in Fore Street were demolished in 1868 enabling the Market House to be extended. Local architect Henry Rice was used on this occasion and the original 1st floor exterior can still be seen today above No. 25 Fore Street.

In celebration of Queen Victoria's coronation on June 28th 1838, six hundred men and boys dined on two bullocks, two hog's heads of cider and two of beer in the Market House. Tea and cakes for one thousand women and children followed. In November 1859 the Volunteer Rifle Corps were allowed by the Town Council to use the top floor as their Drill Hall. When their rifles were not in use P.C. Humphreys would take charge of them.

The Market House prior to demolition in the 1950s

Cornish Times columnist J.K. Broad recalled the building as a boy in the late 1800s, '*in those days it was a veritable hive of industry, the top market was crowded with Farmers' wives from the whole countryside around, vying with one another in the attractiveness of their display. Butter, eggs, ducks and chicken, truly a goodly choice. On the ground floor a chattering bevy of Saltash Fishwives with a delectable show of shrimps, mussels and pickled cockles. A penny entitled one to a tiny dish together with a pin, from the stallholder's matronly bosom, with which to handle these succulent morsels. The Centre Floor, here congregated the fruit and confectionary stalls, fancy goods, toys, stationery and literature. One could purchase pants and vests, trousers and boots and be accommodated with a ham sandwich and a cup of tea*'.

Mr. Pickles's Electric Cinema occupied one of the floors from 1915 to 1934 and being silent movies, he purchased an organ from a chapel in Pensilva for thirty shillings. The first showing on July 21st 1915 was a Navy recruitment film 'The Royal Naval Division at Work and Play'. In the 1930s a resident of Duloe shared his memories of the Electric Cinema, '*the children would sit in the front three or four rows and would be charged 3d. Children then, as now, would become rowdy and the proprietor would come and walk across in front of them cracking a horse whip. If this did not do the trick, he would single out the offenders and crack the whip just a few inches over their heads. He was an expert with that whip. Can you imagine what would happen to anyone if they did that today?*'

LISKEARD'S CRICKETING VICAR

REV. CANON JOHN HENRY PARSONS MC

Born in 1890, Rev. Canon John Henry Parsons MC began his working career racing Humber motor cars for the manufacturer before enlisting for WWI. He was awarded the Military Cross and two swords for gallantry. '*Jack*' had those swords beaten into ploughshares by a Blacksmith, ploughed part of a field with them and two horses, grew wheat and from that made communion bread. The ploughshares are housed in the Worcestershire Yeomanry Military Museum, the company he served in as a Cavalry Officer in Gallipoli, Palestine and India.

Rev. Canon John Henry Parsons M.C

Ordained in 1929, he eventually became Vicar of Liskeard and St. Keyne in 1939, and in the June of that year made one hundred and fifty runs in one innings for Liskeard Cricket Club. This included a six, after which the ball had to be collected from beyond the road to St. Cleer. From 1910 to 1914 '*Jack*' had played as a professional for Warwickshire County Cricket Club and after WWI continued until 1928, when he enrolled at St. Aiden's theological college in Birkenhead. He scored 17,969 runs, which included thirty eight centuries and a top score of two hundred and twenty five. His run average was 35.72 per game. WWII saw Jack back in service, on this occasion with the Royal Army Chaplains' Department in North Africa and Italy, and at the end of the war he returned to Liskeard.

On Nov. 19th 1948 the *Cornish Times* reported that the Rector of St. Keyne was responsible for the upkeep of St. Keyne Holy Well and a trust fund provided £3 per year towards the cost. Due to the untidy state of the well, Rev. J.H. Parsons was questioned on the matter and responded that '*as far as I am concerned I am not the Custodian of the well and I have no intention of being held responsible for its upkeep, as to what has happened to the £3 per year in question, I have not the foggiest idea*'. The dispute was later resolved by Liskeard Old Cornwall Society taking on the Custodian duties.

On the death of Warleggan's eccentric and much maligned Rev. Frederick William Densham in 1953, his body was cremated at Efford in Plymouth and the ashes were scattered there. Solicitor's clerk Mr. Leslie Winder was the one mourner that followed the coffin, representing his employer and Densham's elderly brother Edgar who was unable to attend. The *Cornish Guardian* reported that Canon J.H. Parsons had specifically requested that a funeral service should be held in Cornwall before the cremation in Devon; this was held in St. Martin's Church, Liskeard, officiated by Canon Parsons.

St. Keyne Well

St. Keyne Holy Well maintained annually by Liskeard OCS

Canon Parson's biography 'Cricketer Militant' was published on his 90th birthday, May 30th 1980

In the February 1958 issue of the St. Martin's Club newsletter, it was reported that a Teddy boy was ejected from the Church Hall by club members for being drunk and using bad language. The youth returned later shouting and threatening to knock the vicar's block off, but he was himself floored by the 69 year old vicar, Canon J.H. Parsons. At a later meeting between the Teddy boy and the Vicar, the former apologised for his behaviour and asked if he could join the Club. His apology was accepted and was told *'that the whole affair is behind us'*. His request to join the Club was accepted and the Vicar even paid the boy's first year's subscription.

The Rev. Canon John Henry Parsons MC died at the grand age of 90 in a Plymouth nursing home on February 2nd 1981.

TEMPERANCE HOLLOW
LODGING HOUSE RESIDENTS

One of the two date stones on the Constitutional Club building in Market Street is *'1673 Joseph Upcot'*. The Upcot name appears on land related documents dated 1671, 1676 and 1679 where he is described as a Gentleman of Morval and a Merchant of Liskeard. He is known to have sided with the Parliamentarians in the 1644 Battle of Lostwithiel, so presumably not very popular in staunchly Royalist Liskeard. The other date stone, simply *'1910'*, refers to the opening of the locally abbreviated 'Con Club'.

By 1861 Upcot's home had become a multi-occupied lodging house wedged between Wenmoth the Ironmonger on one side and Edgcumbe the Draper on the other. It was home to several mining families including 44 year old Lead Miner William Hollow, his wife Temperance a year older, and a visitor named Catherine Treloar. Catherine is mentioned in Lesley Trotter's book *The Married Widows of Cornwall*, *'Catherine could confidently be identified as a recipient of a money letter registered at Bruce Mines Post Office in Northern Ontario, Canada between 11th December 1857 and 29th July 1861'*. After 1861 there's no further record of Catherine Treloar in England, so perhaps her money letter contained enough for her passage to Canada and a reunion with her husband Thomas. Also with no record after 1861 is William Hollow; perhaps he was tempted to try life in Canada as well?

The former first floor alms-houses in Church Street South

But Temperance Hollow stayed in Liskeard, in 1881 at age 65 and a Widow, she was *'in service'* at Westbourne House, home to the wealthiest man in Liskeard, whose own mother was *'in service'* before he made his fortune as a Mine Share Broker (see *'Rags to Riches'* on p.48). In addition to Temperance, two Housemaids, a Cook and a Butler were employed by Richard and Sarah Hawke.

The left hand datestone on the Constitutional Club in Market Street

An entry in the Liskeard Union Register tells us that Temperance was unable to work due to infirmity at the age of 73 and was approved to receive Poor Relief on 29th March 1888. It was *"out relief"* that Temperance received as she was living in the former alms-houses in Church Street South, not in the Union Workhouse on Station Road. This is confirmed in the 1901 census which shows Temperance was joined in Church Street South by two others ladies named on the same page of the Union Register: Harriet McLauchlan (Widow at 69) and Sarah May (Unmarried at 70), both also receiving *'out relief'*. The entry in the last column in the Liskeard Union Register, which is preserved in the Liskeard & District Museum, for Temperance Hollow is *'death from of old age on 3rd April 1903'* and, like most others receiving Poor Relief, she'll be in an un-marked pauper's grave somewhere in Liskeard.

Quene outside Willcox & Sons during the 1974 Bread Strike

A BAKERY FOR 156 YEARS

No.6 DEAN STREET

The first census after local Architect Henry Rice designed the Grade II listed No.6 Dean Street was in 1861. Head of the household was 34 year old Baker Thomas White, employing three men and three boys. 42 year old Mary was his wife, their son Charles was 7 and daughter Ellen two years younger. Also living-in were a Journeyman Baker, two Apprentice Bakers, a General Servant and a 13 year old Servant Boy.

On June 2nd 1863 at 37 years old Thomas was initiated into the St. Martin's Masonic Lodge and became their Worshipful Master ten years later, and served as Treasurer for twenty six years. In December 1873 he presented the Lodge with the Worshipful Master's Chair which is still in use today. In his regular *Cornish Times* column, J.K. Broad wrote '*Mr. Thomas White, Baker of Dean Street, was a prominent tradesman who cultivated quite an extensive wholesale business amongst the many traders scattered over the town. Monday morning would find him about the tick, and having taken two pence off, the cash would be gathered in that old cloth bag of his tied with a string, his mouth meanwhile! Was it Wrigley's or a mere chewing of the cud?*'

Another memory from Broad was '*Mr. White the Baker owned some fields near Addington, where he kept ten geese and a gander. Everything went well until, on visiting the fields one morning a week before Christmas, there was only the gander to be seen. Strutting around with something attached to its neck, this was found to be a bag containing ten coppers and a note, which read: 'Toughy White/ We've won the right/ Don't leave your mind to wander/ We've bought your geese/ At a penny a piece/ And left the money with the gander.'*

In 1921 Joseph Willcox bought the Bakery in Dean Street, the price included two four-wheeled wagons, a two-wheeled wagon and three grey horses named Duke, Jo and Lucy. Willcox carried on the contract to supply bread to the Union Workhouse in Station Road, which White had previously undertaken for many years. Every Tuesday and Friday the horse drawn wagons delivered ninety two to ninety eight loaves to the Workhouse, each loaf weighing 4 lbs. The Willcox family running the business in 1939 consisted of Joseph (68, Baker and Confectioner), Laura (67, House and Business Manager), Harold (28, Master Baker) and Ivy (33, Bakery Assistant).

Blakes the Master Bakers occupied the premises from 1980 to 2017, when they moved to the Parade. The one hundred and fifty six years of No.6 Dean Street being a Bakery came to an end when Day Lewis the Chemist arrived in 2017.

Delivery wagon outside the Dean Street Bakery about 1900

THE MARRIED WIDOWS OF ADDINGTON
SARAH PARKYN AND JANE CONGDON

In Addington Place North, Liskeard, in 1871 two ladies living just a few houses apart were wives of miners working abroad, but both had to find work for themselves to supplement the little, if any, money sent home by their husbands. They are both mentioned in Lesley Trotter's book, *The Married Widows of Cornwall*.

In the census of that year Sarah Parkyn, at the age of 43 gave her occupation as '*Laundress, husband working abroad*'. Laundress was, according to Trotter's research, '*low status or last resort, so associated with poverty or distress.*' Sarah's working life had started at the age of 15, or earlier, as a Farm Servant in Colan, Cornwall. The 1861 census tells us that her '*husband working abroad*' was John Parkyn, six years younger than Sarah, a Lead Miner in one of the Menheniot mines two miles from home before he left. The pending closure of these mines in the late 1860s and early 1870s would have prompted John to join the Cornish Diaspora as there is no further record of him in England after that 1861 entry. Sarah never joined her husband as she appears in subsequent censuses in Addington Place North until 1891 when she was aged 65, widowed and still taking in other people's washing.

Cornish Miners in Moonta, South Australia in the 1860s

ADDINGTON NORTH, LISKEARD.

Addington Place North is the terrace on the right

Her neighbour in 1871 was Jane Ann Congdon aged 32, who gave her occupation as 'Nurse, husband a miner in Australia'. Quoting Trotter again, a Nurse was 'not the qualified professional we know today, the only skills they had were what they had been taught within the family'. Also in the census are her sons William (10) and John (8), and Jane Ann's mother Jane Batten (63) who would have helped in the running of the home. At 13 years old Jane Ann had been a live-in Domestic Servant on Trengrove Farm, Menheniot.

The 'husband a miner in Australia' was George Congdon who, at 15 years of age or earlier, had been a Labourer in one of the same Menheniot lead mines as John Parkyn. We know Jane Batten died in 1878, but there is no further record of her daughter or her grandsons. As did many other Cornish miners working abroad, George Congdon hopefully sent enough money home to pay for his wife and sons to join him in Australia to experience a more comfortable existence than her less fortunate neighbour in Addington, Sarah Parkyn, a washer woman until she died.

Victoria Terrace, Station Road, Amy Stanton lived in the 4th house from the left

Liskeard, Victoria Terrace.

EARLY LADY PHOTOGRAPHERS

JESSE DOWLING AND AMY STANTON

Only one mounting card embossed *'Photograph by Dowling & Stanton, Liskeard'* has been located to date, but the photograph the mount borders has produced many strands of local history. It records the laying of the first floor foundation stones of the New Liberal Club on August 23rd 1913, which can still be seen today above The Book Shop in Barras Street. Jesse Dowling was the elder of the two photographers, at 36, unmarried and living with her parents and younger sister in Wadeland Terrace, New Road. At 14 Jesse was *'in service'* to a 75 year old Widow, at 24 she was employed as a Photographic Assistant and at 34 had become a self-employed Photographer.

Amy Stanton was 26 when the New Liberal Club photograph was taken, having been born in Hong Kong in 1887 where her father William was a Police Inspector. William's obituary in the *Cornish Times* of December 31st 1909 tells us that in his youth he worked at South Caradon Mine near Crow's Nest. On reaching manhood William joined the Metropolitan Police, then, in 1873 aged 24, he sailed to Hong Kong to join the Colonial police force. During his twenty five years' service he embraced the Chinese culture about which he wrote several books. His mastering of the language enabled him to be an Interpreter for the Governor, who presented him with a gold watch and chain after he solved a series of organised crimes against the Chinese Government. William returned to Cornwall in 1898 with his two daughters and devoted his time to local affairs for the good of the community. In evidence of this, his funeral, in St. Cleer Churchyard on December 29th 1909, was attended by the Mayor of Liskeard and many prominent local dignitaries.

The laying of the Liberal Club foundation stones on August 23rd 1913,
photograph by Dowling & Stanton

By 1911 the Stanton daughters, both born in Hong Kong, were residing at No.4 Victoria Terrace, Station Road: Emily (29) unmarried having private means and Amy (24) also unmarried and a self-employed photographer. Their cousin Mary (31) was their unmarried domestic help. It's interesting to note that next door but one to the ladies lived John Sparks Elliott, the building contractor for the New Liberal Club, and next door to him lived Elizabeth Priscilla Millman, wife of Liberal Agent C.A. Millman, who laid one of the foundation stones and can be seen on the scaffold in the 1913 Dowling & Stanton photograph. Perhaps Amy's neighbours gave the ladies a career boost by appointing them Official Photographers for the grand ceremony.

Amy married George Doo and left Liskeard to run a Boarding House in West London where their son, William Stanton Doo was born in June 1927. Amy and George returned to Hong Kong in May 1937, leaving young William with his Aunt Emily at 4 Victoria Terrace. An additional inscription to William Stanton's headstone in St. Cleer Churchyard reads '*Also in memory of his daughter Amy presumed killed by enemy action in Singapore February 1942 aged 55 years*'.

THE ROACH FAMILY BIBLE

An Illustrated National Family Bible weighing 12lbs 8oz and measuring 12"x10"x3" with metal clasps can be seen in the Liskeard Old Cornwall Society archive in Stuart House. It contains the message *'Mary Elizabeth Mabel Roach from her loving Mother M.E. Roach'*. By the same hand Edward Roach has been written under the heading *'Honour thy Father'* and Mary Ellen Roach under *'And thy Mother'*. There is a second entry in different, younger handwriting; Edward Roach again for Father, but just Mary Roach for Mother.

Edward was born in Modbury, Devon in 1861 and married Mary Ellen Millett in 1889. Mary Elizabeth Mabel Roach was born in 1892 and was followed 2 years later, in 1894 by a brother Edward John Roach. 1894 is the presentation date in the Family Bible, but in the March of that year Mabel, as she was known, tragically lost her mother during childbirth at just 33 years old.

A page from the Roach Family Bible

Edward senior, at 40 and a widower, remarried in September 1900 to Mary Sowden and began employment with the Martyn family at Tremeddan House, Liskeard, as Coachman, Groom and Gardener. The family lived nearby at Greenbank Cottages on the Tremeddan estate. In 1901 the family members were Edward (40), Mary (46), Mary E.M. (9), Edward J. (7) and Edward's stepsons John T. Sowden (Groom aged 19) and Fred Sowden (Apprentice Builder aged 18).

About this time Mabel would have made the second entry in her Bible under '*And thy Mother*', i.e. Mary Roach. Mabel left school at 12 to work as a Tweeny, (a Maid between floors) at Stuart House, now home to her heavyweight Bible. When Greenbank Cottages were demolished for road widening Mabel was rehoused in one of the many '*prefabs*' which were once where the Liskeard School Sports Fields are today.

Surviving in Liskeard & District Museum are the original certificates to mark Mabel's admission to the National Association Friendly Society on her 21st birthday and her enrolment to the Civil Defence Corps in 1952. She received a long service medal from the Women's Voluntary Service and was a stalwart of the Darby and Joan Club. Mary Elizabeth Mabel Roach died aged 96 at her home in Melbourne Road in July 1988.

Edward Roach, Coachman at Tremeddan House

SHAMBLES AND FIREFIGHTERS

THE GUILDHALL

The *Cornish Times* of October 1st 1859 contained extensive coverage of the opening of the Guildhall on the corner of Fore Street and Pike Street, the site of the old Town Hall which had included the defunct Tin Court, since 1574. The plans were supplied by the London based Surveyor of County Courts Charles Reeves and the construction was overseen by local Architect Henry Rice. The contractors, principally using granite from the Cheesewring Quarry, included Samuel Bone, whose initials can still be seen today on the Guildhall weather vane. The opening celebrations included an afternoon tea for two hundred elderly ladies of the town, an excellent and substantial dinner for one hundred and seventy three guests provided by Mr. Littleton of the Bell Hotel, a concert by the amateur performers of the Borough and finally, a grand Evening Ball.

The weather vane atop the Guildhall displaying SB and 1859

The whole of the ground floor housed the meat market or Shambles. The Mayor of Liskeard Matthew Loam signed, sealed and delivered the following rental agreement on behalf of the Borough: '*I, Samuel Penny of the Borough of Liskeard in the County of Cornwall, Butcher do hereby agree to take, and we, the said Mayor, Aldermen and Burgesses of the Borough of Liskeard, aforesaid, do hereby agree to let Stall Number 22 in the said Shambles from the ninth day of November 1870 to the eighth day of November 1871 at the weekly rent of three shillings and three pence.*'

In that year of 1871 Matthew Loam engaged Henry Rice to design and erect a monument on the Parade to his father Michael who had recently died. Rice's fee was £100 and The Fountain, with a horse's drinking trough in front, are still prominent in the town centre. Michael Loam was the Mining Engineer who was awarded a prize in 1841 by the Royal Cornwall Polytechnic Society for the best model of a machine for lifting miners to the surface of a shaft. An engine based on Loam's design was built soon after at Tresavean Mine, it became known as the Man-Engine and went on to save the lives of many thousands of miners in years to come.

The Guildhall on the corner of Fore Street and Pike Street

Mr. Samuel Penny of Maudlin was remembered by *Cornish Times* columnist J.K. Broad, as *'a genial old fellow of noble proportions. In the prosperous days of our meat market, he was perhaps the most conspicuous figure of the whole assembly. How vividly one recalls that benignant smile, as diving into his capacious pocket for the change, he sometimes fetched out an odd copper for myself.'*

In later years some of the stalls gave way to the Liskeard Fire Brigade to house their engine. Rule number three in their 1889 Rule Book was *'The Foreman shall be paid the yearly salary of £4, the Assistant Foreman £2 and the Messenger £1. Each other member of the Brigade who shall be present at a Fire the sum of 5s.'* The Town Council provided each member of the Brigade with a Helmet, Tunic, Waterproof Leggings, Belt, Hatchet and Spanner.

The 1860s saw the Guildhall attacked by stone-throwing mobs trying to disrupt meetings of the new Teetotal Society

BUTTON MOON

THOMAS MOON THE TAILOR

Metal-detectorist Mike Burke recently uncovered a button in the St. Just area with 'T.E. Moon Liskeard' stamped on it. Thomas Moon opened his Tailor shop in Tavern Hill, now Pike Street, about 1840 and 4 years later had moved to larger premises at No.1 Fore Street where the Moons traded for over 50 years. The link with St. Just is that Thomas's wife Elizabeth was born in St. Just in Penwith in about 1800, perhaps the button was mislaid on a visit to her family?

In 1838 Thomas Moon was instrumental as a Trustee, in raising funds by public subscription to build the chapel in Greenbank Road for the Wesleyan Methodist Association. It was in 1843 that Thomas engaged his first apprentice, John May, son of an Agricultural Labourer. John, at the age of 14, agreed that for the next 7 years '*he shall not commit fornication nor contract matrimony, nor play at cards or dice tables, nor haunt Taverns or Playhouses*'. In return he would be '*instructed in the Art of a Tailor*' receiving 1s 6d per week initially and rising in stages to 5s per week in year seven. In 1851 there were one hundred and two apprentices in Liskeard, fourteen of them to Tailors, but by 1871 John May was himself a Tailor with his own business in Church Street.

In 1851 the Moon family living above the Fore Street shop consisted of Thomas (40, Mercer & Tailor), Elizabeth (51, wife), John M. (18, Mercer's son), Mary (16), Elizabeth (14), Thomas E. (10) and Samuel H. (7). The last four named were all Scholars. At an auction in Webb's Hotel on The Parade on August 23rd 1855, Thomas Moon, Mercer, was able to buy for £740 the two dwelling houses, shops, barn, workshop, garden and stable that he had been previously renting in Fore Street. Business must have been good! Now a man of property, Thomas had a pamphlet printed by his neighbour J. Philp, founder of the *Cornish Times*, titled '*To the Burgesses of the Borough of Liskeard*'. The purpose of the pamphlet was to canvass for votes: '*having been nominated for one (Burgess) of the Town Council of this Borough, I solicit your support, if you think me a suitable person*'. The appeal was successful!

Mike Burke's 2021 photograph of the T.E. Moon button

When Thomas died in 1880 his son, Thomas Edward Moon, whose name appeared on Mike Burke's button, inherited the business. A photograph taken in 1887 of a revival by children of the '*Mayor Mocking*' tradition for Queen Victoria's Golden Jubilee, clearly shows in the background the sign '*T.E. Moon's Drapery & Cloth Warehouse*' attached to the side wall of No.1 Fore Street. The photograph has been reproduced on the front cover of this book

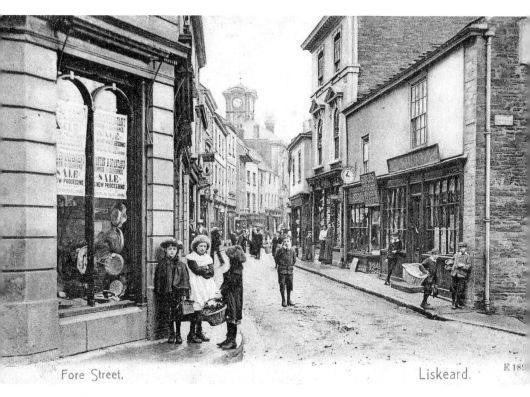

Fore Street.   Liskeard.   E 189

T.E. Moon's Shop was far right in c.1900 Fore Street.

Joseph Hoare, a poor orphan of the Parish, was apprenticed at the age of seven to learn the art of Husbandry from William Dawe in 1813

The full extent of the Moon's services in 1888 were Linen & Woollen Draper, Tailor & General Outfitter, Hosier & Haberdasher, Funerals Furnished and Liveries Provided. A complete set of best clothes cost £3 14s and a pair of gloves 3s 6d. Thomas E. Moon's last entry in a Trade Directory was in 1893 when he was employing seven men and two boys. He was aged 52, unmarried and living above the shop, together with his siblings Mary (57, Housekeeper) and Samuel (49, Draper), who were also unmarried. All three, as well as their mother Elizabeth are buried together in Lanchard Cemetery, Station Road.

41

THE TRAGIC HEADSTONES OF
HICKS AND HUGO

The following inscription can be seen on a granite headstone in Lanchard Cemetery in Station Road, *'underneath repose the remains of Francis Hicks of this town who was killed by the falling of a block of granite while he superintended the erection of the Town Hall August the 20th 1858 aged 46 years'*. In Liskeard in 1837 Francis, a Mason by trade, married Sally Perry, a Straw Bonnet Maker, both were originally from Polperro. By 1851 they were living in Pound Street with their sons Thomas (12), John (9) and William (4).

In 1861, three years after the unexpected death of the breadwinner, the Hicks family seemed to be managing reasonably well; Sally (50) was still making bonnets in Pound Street, William (14) was apprenticed to a Printer's Compositor, John (19) was a Tailor's apprentice and Thomas (22) was a Certified Schoolmaster, living away from home. By the age of 60, Sally had retired and moved to Poole in Dorset to live with her eldest son Thomas, now a British Schoolmaster, her daughter-in-law Martha and her four grandchildren. A nice ending to the tragic story engraved on Francis Hicks' headstone.

Francis Hicks' headstone in Lanchard Cemetery, Station Road

Lanchard Cemetery was opened in 1847 for Dissenters, a centre plot cost one guinea, or six shillings in the borders.

Another tragic event is recorded on a
headstone in St. Martin's Churchyard,
*'To the memory of Richard Hugo of this
Borough who was accidently killed by the
falling of a wall when passing the Post Office
corner on the 9th day of June 1864 aged 39
years'*. In his early teens Richard was
employed as a live-in Servant by a
Farmer in St. Keyne. At the time of his
demise he was a Servant to Solicitor
John Sargent of Parade House. He left
his wife, Elizabeth, a widow at 33 years
old with six children to support.

In 1867 Elizabeth remarried, to Daniel
Gumb, a Miner who also farmed five
acres near Trewidland. Her
childbearing duties continued; by 1881
Elizabeth (48) and Daniel (52) were
living on North Meadow Farm,
Norton, Durham with their daughter
Bessie (12) and son Fred (10). Daniel's
occupation was Farm Labourer which
makes it difficult to imagine why they
should undertake, for those times, such
a huge journey to re-locate.
Considering the Hugo family's
circumstances, where did the money
come from to pay for Richard's
headstone, made even more expensive
than usual because of all those extra
letters? John Bone, the Post Office
demolition contractor, at the inquest,
escaped official blame for the falling of
the wall, but in an attempt to restore
his failing reputation in the town, he
paid for the funeral expenses, as well as
those of the two 5 year boys who also
died in the same tragic accident.

*Richard Hugo's headstone in
St. Martin's Churchyard*

DR. MARRACK'S BRONCHIAL MIXTURE

MANLEY TERRACE

The first census after the building of the prestigious Manley Terrace in Station Road Liskeard was in 1871. The architect was the prolific and highly respected local man Henry Rice. In residence at No.8 were 40 year old practising surgeon William Marrack W.R.C.S., L.S.A., his wife Lydia (32) and daughters Mary (7) and Edith (6). Live-in Domestic Servants were Catherine Snell (22, Cook) and Mary Stephens (24, Housemaid). Three sons followed later; John, Richard and George, George became a surgeon like his father.

In the following December the *Cornish Times* reported that a '*storm broke with great violence over this town and the damage was considerable. At Manley Terrace a chimney 12 feet high of the end house occupied by Mr. Marrack, surgeon, was blown down and fell with great force through the roof of the room below carrying with it the cemented cornice weighing 5 cwt. There was about 3 or 4 tons of debris deposited on the floor of the front bedroom*'. Mrs Marrack had just left the bedroom so fortunately there were no injuries.

It was about this time that Dr. Marrack's Bronchial Mixture could be purchased for 1s ½d from William H. Wearing's chemist shop on the Parade. In fact the shop was in another Henry Rice building at No.4 Pike Street, but the Parade sounded much more up market! Advertisements claimed the mixture to be '*the noted cure for coughs, colds, bronchitis, asthma and influenza*'.

Young & Son ad from 1909

By 1900 Richard Young had taken over the chemist shop and he claimed that the mixture '*has been in use for 40 years. Thousands have proved its efficacy. Contains no opiates. Is perfectly safe.*' It was manufactured by Young & Son, but could be purchased from any of seventeen agents across South East Cornwall from Lostwithiel to Gunnislake. It was also stocked by the Co-operative Societies at Tremar Coombe, Dobwalls and St. Neot.

Described by one of his daughters as '*an awkward character and very difficult to live with*', Dr. Marrack died in Worthing, Sussex, at the age of 68. Another relation told the story of '*a man suffering with lockjaw came to see Dr. William Marrack. The doctor took him upstairs and abruptly pushed him down the stairs. The patient fell and broke his arm but his lockjaw was cured*'.

"At Manley Terrace a chimney 12 feet high of the end house occupied by Mr. Marrack, surgeon, was blown down and fell with great force through the roof of the room below"

Manley Terrace with Gas Lamppost, No.8 is far left

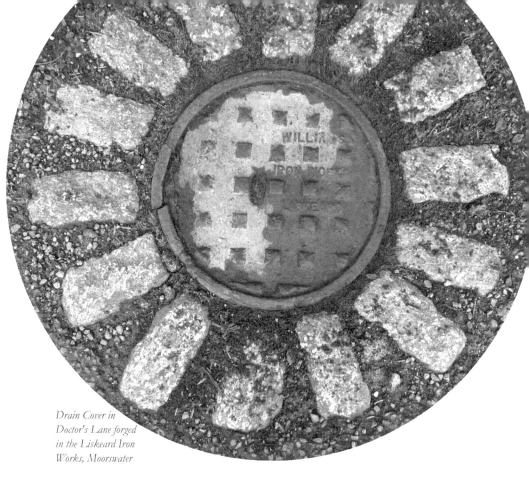

Drain Cover in Doctor's Lane forged in the Liskeard Iron Works, Moorswater

DRY PAVEMENTS & PERFECT FEEDING PENS
IRON WORKS AT MOORSWATER

The first written reference to the Iron Works at Moorswater on the site of an old Corn Mill, and before that a Paper Mill, was in the Cornish Times on June 1st 1861: '*A destructive fire took place between 4 and 5 at Mr. Williams' foundry. Before assistance could be procured, the whole building and its contents were destroyed*'. Just one month later the following announcement appeared: '*Z. Williams most respectfully acquaints his friends in the neighbourhood that he has erected a new foundry at Moorswater on the site of the one recently destroyed by fire, and he is now prepared to execute, with despatch any orders that may be kindly sent to him*'. Born in Perranaworthal in 1818, Zacharias Tregonowen Williams first appeared locally in 1841, and again in 1851, as a Blacksmith lodging in the village of Crow's Nest. He probably worked in the hugely successful South Caradon Mine which was only a ten minute walk from his home. In August 1864, when *'Zach'* was trading from Moorswater as Liskeard Iron Works, he supplied '*bucket joints and hoops, and a ruler*' to his previous employer.

Examples of his other products can still be seen in Liskeard today. Cast iron gullies, which carry rainwater from the gutters' downpipes under pavements, are plentiful in Church Street. With attractive stone surrounds, drain covers are visible in Doctor's Lane and Varley Lane. Iron ramps are still protecting the kerb outside the Barley Sheaf from damage by brewery delivery vehicles. All these products are embossed with '*Williams, Liskeard*'.

An advertisement from December 21st 1861 advised that there was '*always in stock a large assortment of Cooking Stoves of every size, and of the most useful and economical construction, warranted to work with half less fuel than those of ordinary make, are free from dust, a perfect cure for smoky chimneys and an ornament to any kitchen*'. At various times during renovation work these stoves, with the mark '*Z.T. Williams, Liskeard*', have been uncovered at No.1 Barn Street, No.3 Fore Street and in Lamellion Farmhouse.

When Zach died in 1877 his son Richard continued his father's business, and in May 1890 he purchased for £40 from the Borough of Liskeard '*all that piece of land with the old building there-on commonly called or known by the name of Lady Well, situate in Church Street in the said Borough*'. Richard replaced the old building with an extensive showroom which he stocked with household products such as kettles, saucepans, irons and those cooking stoves. The building, at No.6 Church Street is now occupied by an advice centre, at one time there was a spiral staircase with steps that were forged in Moorswater. An important source of business for Richard was

gradually disappearing with the closures of the mines in the Caradon District in the 1870s and 1880s, business that needed to be replaced. The Liskeard Iron Works catalogues of the time were designed to attract the farming community by giving their machinery some imaginative names: '*The Invincible double furrow plough, The Champion turn-wrest plough, the Criterion single furrow plough and the Perfection cattle feeding pen*'.

Historian Jack Haworth examining a Williams stove in Lamellion Farmhouse

RAGS TO RICHES
RICHARD AND SARAH HAWKE

Supported by newspaper articles and censuses this is the most remarkable *'rags to riches'* story in Liskeard history. It is of Richard Hawke (1823-1887), of Grade II Listed Westbourne House in West Street. In 1841 at the age of 18 Richard was an apprentice barber in Helston, his mother was *'in service'* and no mention of a father. However, by 1851 he owned a Barber Shop in Fore Street, Liskeard employing one man and an apprentice, he was married to Sarah and his mother, no longer in service, was living with them above the shop.

The monument above Richard and Sarah Hawke's ashes in the 1950s

Hawke was also Mine Barber at the nearby hugely successful South Caradon Mine. The story is that he overheard miners discussing possible promising new copper seams, he bought a few shares while they were cheap and made a good profit when the seams proved to be successful. Before long the mine owners, Peter and James Clymo recognised Hawke's talent and appointed him to be their share dealer in London. After branching out on his own as a Mine Share Broker, and advertising his services in The Mining Journal, he soon made enough money to buy Westbourne, the grandest house in Liskeard, at only 35 years of age.

In 1861 Hawke employed the only Butler in Liskeard, 57 year old Thomas Munday, and his mother, the former servant, is described in the census as a Gentlewoman. Richard Hawke died in 1887 the wealthiest man in Liskeard, his estate in today's values being about £16million. On Sarah's death in 1904 the estate went to Solicitor William Sargent, grandson of a Liskeard Cordwainer, who the childless Hawkes regarded as their adopted son. Their original choice of heir had been Peter Conyngham Glubb, eldest son of their neighbours in Pendean House. Their mind was changed when Conyngham, as he was known, became something of a wastrel, refusing to work and sponging off his relations.

Richard Hawke (1823-1887)

In 1887 cremation had only been legal for four years and, on Hawkes's instruction, his body was transported by train to Woking Crematorium, one of the few licensed establishments in the country. It was Sargent who accompanied Hawke's body and returned to Liskeard with the ashes in an ornamental box. One hundred of Liskeard's worthies received invitations on gilt edged cards to attend the interment of the ashes on November 22nd 1887. They gathered in the reception room of Westbourne, recited the Lord's Prayer then formed a procession to walk, with headwear removed, to the lower part of the gardens. As no '*man of the cloth*' was present, at Hawke's request, the procession was led by his friend and physician Mr. Hingston of Rosedean Surgery. A few words were said and the box was placed in a small vault, leaving space enough for the ashes of Sarah Hawke, over which a fine granite memorial stone was erected, which still stands and has a Grade II listing. The *Western Morning News* report the following day confirmed that '*the rain was pouring all the time*' of the ceremony.

A CAPITAL HOTEL AND A TAP ROOM

WEBB'S HOTEL

As its date stone confirms Webb's Hotel was built in 1833, and was described at the time as *'this new and capital hotel on the Parade'*. The stone also bears the initials of the first owner Richard Webb. Webb had previously been landlord of the King's Arms in Pike Street on a site now occupied by the Liskeard & District Museum. His father William Webb was the landlord before him, having previously been Butler to Edward, Lord Eliot of St. Germans whose town house was in Castle Street, Liskeard.

Such was its reputation, that the King of Saxony stayed at Webb's in 1846 and it became the terminus for several mail and stagecoach services. In 1852 the Royal Mail Coach that left Webb's at 8.45am would arrive in Falmouth at 4.30pm on the same day, having stopped at Bodmin and Truro en-route.

There was a seedier side to Webb's however, mostly in connection with the Tap Room accessed via Tavern Hill (now Pike Street). In April 1844 Selina Collins (20) and Joanna May (19) had been hanging around Webb's Tap, when they accosted (soliciting would be the word used now) Sam Hender from St. Cleer during which they stole his watch. Collins was deported for seven years and May imprisoned for six months. Joanna May hadn't learnt her lesson as two years later she was imprisoned again, this time for ten years. Outside Webb's Tap again, she accosted mine agent Mark Matthews then stole his silk handkerchief and £14 10s.

Webb's Hotel on the Parade in 1890

The Mayor's Parade passing Webb's Tap in Pike Street in 1962

Victory in Europe was announced from the Webb's Hotel balcony to a huge crowd on May 8th 1945

The 1930s saw the opening of a large ballroom in the rear of the ground floor, one of the first grand balls to be held was a *'Dinner and Dance, Webb's Hotel Liskeard, New Year's Eve, 1937'*. The message alongside the menu was, *'The end of 1937 and the opening of 1938 coincides with the beginning of a New Era in the history of Webb's Hotel, in which all that is worthy of preservation of the Past will be allied to the ever changing improvements of the Present'*. I wonder if any of the guests thought the printing of the menu all in French, with no translation, was an improvement?

Local soft drinks manufacturer Mr. G.A. Crinks (Crinks for Drinks being his slogan) purchased Webb's Hotel at a Public Auction for £17,600 in 1945. After over forty years of successful trading the Crinks family decided to sell up, but customers were greeted by this unusually direct message on display in the door window: *'10 November 1989, we regret that due to the Financial Failure by Mr. N.G.A. Hastings to complete the purchase of this property, the business of this Hotel is closed as from the above date'*. The Bailiffs arriving to enforce the eviction of Hastings were watched by the Press, the Crinks family and many interested onlookers, two weeks later Webb's was advertised for sale once again.

One of these cottages in Lower Lux Street, demolished in 1967, was the home of the Brown family

LOWER LUX STREET TO WEXFORD COUNTY
SARAH BROWN AND SAMUEL HICKS

Sarah Brown had some interesting neighbours when she was growing up in a now demolished tiny cottage in Lower Lux Street with her three brothers and four sisters. Nearby was the old Globe Inn where a Joseph Hancock was *'acting in a riotous manner and refusing to leave'*, he was fined five shillings by the Magistrates. The following month the landlord himself was fined for *'allowing drunk and disorderly conduct'*. In an adjoining cottage to the Browns, William O'Bryan, a founder of the Bible Christian movement, formerly known as the Bryanites, was licenced to hold prayer meetings there until the Bible Christians built their own Chapel in Barn Street in 1854, which later became the Liskeard Silver Band room. Meetings in Lower Lux Street were sometimes disrupted by rude boys blowing pepper through the keyhole causing much annoyance to the worshippers inside.

At the age of 18 in 1851 Sarah had left home, she was lodging in nearby Higher Lux Street and working as a Mine Girl in one of the new copper mines around Caradon Hill. On February 28th 1862 the *West Briton* reported that *'a 17 year old Bal Maiden went to work at South Caradon Mine a little late in the morning. To escape being seen by the Captain, she went into the jigging house instead of going through the tool house as usual. By some means she got her dress caught in the coupling of the jigging machine, by which means she was crushed to death'*. Sarah avoided such accidents and two years later she married Samuel Hicks, a 22-year-old Lead Miner from Crowan, near Camborne. In 1861 they were living in one of the rows of cramped

Crow's Nest Wesleyan Chapel, possibly attended by the Hicks family

cottages off Higher Lux Street with an outside privy and a shared stand pipe for running water; too early for gas or electricity. Known as Courts they were hastily erected to house the influx of miners arriving from West Cornwall seeking employment during the Caradon copper boom. Additions to the Hicks family in 1861 were Lucy (8), Mary (6) and John (1).

After that 1861 census there is no further record of Samuel Hicks in England, but Sarah in 1871 was living in Darite Terrace, Crow's Nest, with her three children, two of whom were contributing to the family income: Lucy (18) was a Tailor and Mary (16) a Dressmaker. So where was Samuel Hicks? Samuel had in fact become part of the great Cornish Diaspora, but unlike thousands of others he had the sense to obtain a contract of employment with the Central Mine in Michigan. The contract included part of his wages being sent home to support the family he left behind. This is confirmed in records held at the Royal Institute of Cornwall which show that in October 1876, Sarah Hicks of St. Cleer Parish received a remittance from the Central Mine in Michigan, U.S.A. via the Manchester and County Bank (information from Lesley Trotter's book *The Married Widows of Cornwall*).

After that 1871 census there is no further record of Samuel's wife and children in England, but in the 1880 census for Sherman, Wexford County, Michigan, USA are Samuel Hicks, born England 1831 and Sarah, born England 1832. Hopefully they enjoyed a better life than in Liskeard, but at the very least the family were reunited.

BOOKWORMS AND THE BEDRIDDEN

JOHN PASSMORE EDWARDS

In 1895 John Passmore Edwards, the Cornish Philanthropist, agreed to pay for the building of a hospital and a library in Liskeard, and then donated both to the town. This was subject to the Borough Council agreeing to fund the future running of both institutions, and that suitable locations could be provided. For the Cottage Hospital, land at Barras Cross was gifted by Lewis Carrington Marshall out of his Treworgey Manor estates. His name can be seen on one of the two foundation stones. The man who laid the stones on May 21st 1895, using a silver trowel, was Lord Mount Edgcumbe, Lord Lieutenant and Deputy Grand Master of the Freemasons of England. The ceremony took place after a procession of over two hundred Freemasons, in full regalia, arrived in Barras Cross having set off from the Temperance Hall in Barn Street.

The honorary medical staff included Dr Nettle of Parade House, Dr Hammond of Stuart House and Dr Hingston of Rosedean House. The honorary dentist was W.H. Lyne of Trion House. The poor of Liskeard were treated free of charge and those who could afford it, paid up to two guineas. A report on the sixty-six patients treated in 1899 stated that forty-five were cured, six were much improved, three were '*relieved*' and six sadly died. The fate of the remaining six wasn't given. Major improvements came in 1927: an operating theatre, X-ray apparatus, nurses' quarters and, at long last, electricity.

The other foundation stone at the hospital bears the name of Mrs. Passmore Edwards, who '*cut the ribbon*' on April 28th 1896. On the same day that Mrs. Edwards opened the

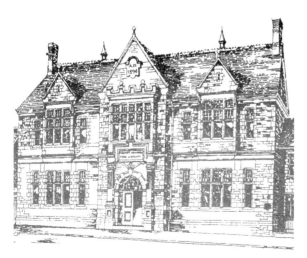

Cottage Hospital, Mr. Edwards laid the foundation stone for the Passmore Edwards Library in Barras Street, Liskeard. During the excavation, in the former gardens of Stuart House, the workmen discovered a lead/silver lode running from North to South and measuring 2 feet wide. The lode was 7 feet below the surface and some fine mineral samples were taken from it before being sealed over.

An early sketch of the Passmore Edwards Library in Barras Street

The laying of the foundation stones of Liskeard Cottage Hospital in 1895

Although Edwards had met the construction costs, certain members of the Borough Council were concerned as to how they could raise the £200 required for furnishings and fittings. The lack of funding continued, a part-time librarian was paid just £14 a year, and the ground floor had to be let to what later became the National Provincial Bank, until as late as 1954. The Borough also had to contend with objections from the Library Rejection Association, who complained that the library had '*to be upheld at the expense of the ratepayers, for lazy fiction reading people*'.

Edwards returned to open the library, which he dedicated to the former MP Charles Buller, on October 28th 1896 with a silver key. On the same occasion he was presented with a silver casket containing a certificate which confirmed his Freedom of the Borough of Liskeard. After the

opening ceremony a Tea Treat was provided for the poor, infirm, workhouse inmates and children of the Borough. This was followed by an evening of entertainment for the adults, which included a rendition of '*The Gay Tomtit*' and a farce entitled '*The Amorous Policeman, or the Beggar's Revenge*'.

A bust of Charles Buller was presented to the library by Edwards in 1905, which was unveiled by another former MP, Leonard Courtney. The bust is currently on display in the Public Rooms in West Street, Liskeard. In the year 2000 a magnificent mural depicting events from Liskeard's history, the work of local artist June Cole, was unveiled in the library. The mural measures 25 feet by 13 feet and is on the wall alongside the staircase leading to the first floor.

TEMPERANCE HOTELS

Members of the Moon family outside their Temperance Hotel in Barras Street

At a sale by auction in 1855 of fifty seven properties, part of the estate of Samuel Trehawke Kekewich, held in Webb's Hotel on the Parade, Mr. William Moon purchased a dwelling house and garden in Barrel Street (now Barras Street) for £260. Moon later opened his Temperance Hotel there and advertised '*horses and carriages for hire, well aired beds and good stabling*'.

In January 1918 the *Cornish Times* reported that '*Cecilia Grace Moon, daughter of Mrs. Moon of the Temperance Hotel and the late Mr. W. Moon had met a terrible death at the GWR Station*'. Cecilia was aged just 21 and had visited a cousin in Barn Street in the evening, but did not return home. '*She was found by a shunter at the station on the railway line just after 10.00pm. The body was about six feet from the bridge where there was a drop of about 56 feet*'. Her coat was found on the bridge, but no note. At the inquest the cousin said that £55 in gold had gone missing from her house earlier in that week, and PC Burroughs confirmed that the deceased had been spending a good deal of money in gold recently in Liskeard. The jury returned a verdict of Felo-De Se (death by one's own hand).

No.4 Bay Tree Hill, currently Bradleys Estate Agents and previously Purdy's Bakery, appears in Trade Directories until 1892 as the Union Inn. The last landlord, John Brokenshire appeared before the Magistrates on a regular basis. In September 1873 he was fined £2 for allowing card playing in the Union, and in 1887 he was fined five shillings for being drunk on the King's Highway and being a regular offender! His customers were just as bad; John Pearn of Duloe was fined for being drunk and refusing to leave the Union in June 1880, and Richard Wilton of St. Neot was imprisoned for one month for stealing a belt belonging to a recruiting Corporal of the Scots Guards at the Union in November 1873.

In April 1892 a group of thirteen subscribers, including Traders, Merchants, Engineers, a Schoolmaster and an Assurance Agent, formed the Liskeard Temperance Hotel Company Limited and their hotel soon replaced the inn at 4 Bay Tree Hill. Their advertisement offered '*every accommodation for cyclists, a 10 minute walk from the Station, and stabling, Manager: Joseph Deacon*'.

On June 11th 1909 the *Cornish Times* reported that '*Through the prompt action of PC Pooley, stationed at Liskeard, a smart capture was effected at Saltash on Monday evening of a lad, about 16 years of age, who had got away from the Temperance Hotel, Liskeard, with a cash box containing £10 9s 7d. It appears that he arrived in the town on Thursday night, and giving the name of Frank Hill, said he had come from Plymouth, where his parents lived, for a holiday. He appeared to have plenty of money and paid regularly for his board and lodging*'. It was revealed in Court that the lad had given a false name and two false addresses, when in fact he came from a good home in Torquay. Some of the reasons his father suggested for this out of character behaviour were that '*when young he was thrown out of a perambulator*', and that since his son had left home he had '*discovered a lot of Penny Dreadfuls hidden away*'.

Penny Dreadfuls were cheap popular sensational publications containing stories of the exploits of detectives, criminals and supernatural entities. Frank Mildren, his real name, was bound over by the Magistrates in the sum of £5 to be of good behaviour for twelve months.

The Temperance Hotel in Bay Tree Hill in 1919

WOODCARVINGS AND ATTORNEYS
PENDEAN HOUSE

Living at Pendean House in West Street were Albert Charles Lyne Glubb and his son Albert de Castro Glubb. Both were Attorneys at Law, both served as Mayors of Liskeard and they shared a passion for woodcarving. An extremely ornate bookcase can be seen in the Pendean House library with initials and a date, '*ACLG Read Mark Learn and Inwardly Digest 1862*'. The magnificently carved staircase is a true work of art. Kelly's Directory of 1873 lists A.C.L. Glubb as '*solicitor, perpetual commissioner to administer oaths in chancery & stannaries of Cornwall, clerk to the Guardians & sanitary board, clerk to the highway board, superintendent registrar & agent for the West of England Fire & Life Office*'.

Albert de Castro Glubb,
Mayor of Liskeard 1904 to 1906

The Cornish Times on January 21st 1910 reported that a car '*whilst turning the curve just below Dean Terrace, the driver noticed Mr. A.C.L. Glubb walking up the middle of the road*' who '*hesitated which side of the road to take and that the driver was consequently put in a quandary. Suddenly Mr. Glubb made for the pavement and the driver was forced to make a sudden turn to the right to avoid running him down. The wheels of the car went over a granite stone, a Mr. Jago was thrown out of the car and one of the mudguards was smashed, a tyre punctured and the steering rod broken*'. Total cost of the damage was £10, but nobody suffered serious injury.

By the 1911 census A. de C. Glubb was head of the household at Pendean House. His wife Oona at 28 was 17 years his junior and their 7 month old daughter Frances was looked after by live-in Nurse Lily Pitcher from Devonport. In the kitchen was Cook Edith Jane from North Hill. Another passion of Bertie, as he was known to his family, was the restoration and preservation of Cornish antiquities in his capacity of first President of Liskeard Old Cornwall Society from 1928. He and the Society were responsible for rescuing numerous misused ancient Cornish Crosses, Holy Wells, Bridges and pre-history monuments, examples being Trethevy Quoit, King Doniert's Stone, St. Keyne Well and The Hurlers stone circles.

Oona Glubb was born in Marlborough, New Zealand, a granddaughter of James Edward Fitzgerald, the first Canterbury Pilgrim to set foot in New Zealand and is referred to as the country's first Prime Minister. Oonah met Bertie on a short trip to Surrey to visit her Aunt Amy. She never returned to New Zealand apart from a short trip after the death of their son Peter while at Charterhouse boarding school. Oonah was terribly distressed when the school returned Peter's clothes to her, unwashed. It is thought that Oonah was behind the many apparently Maori influenced carvings on the Pendean staircase. Frances was the only surviving child of Bertie and Oonah and her daughter Jenifer Roberts has been generous in providing the author with much information about the Glubbs and Pendean House. Jenifer certainly shares her grandfather Bertie's interest in history having published several books on the subject, including a biography of Oonah's grandfather entitled '*Fitz*'.

A Town Council proposal to compulsory purchase Pendean for their offices in 1947, was refused after a public outcry led by irate ratepayers.

Staircase woodcarvings in Pendean House, West Street

IN THE FACE ADVERSITY
MATHESON FAMILY

Having previously lived in Islington, London, where he worked as a Railway Agent, by 1861 Donald Oliver Matheson had settled into a newly built cottage, No.2 Castle Gardens overlooking Castle Park. With his wife Mary, daughters Rose and Harriet and sons Frederick and Frank, Donald would have witnessed the celebrations that took place in the Park on the occasion of the marriage of the then Duke of Cornwall in 1863, later to become King Edward VII. A traditional Cornish Tea Treat was enjoyed by over two thousand adults and children, which included a roasted bullock, followed by fireworks and a bonfire.

With Donald working as an Inspector of Public Works and the children all at school the Matheson family appeared to have adapted to life in Liskeard after the hustle and bustle of city life in London. However, things took a turn for the worse on December 22nd 1864 when Donald, at the age of 51, was admitted to Bodmin Lunatic Asylum, where he stayed until he died on May 3rd 1866. Six days later his body was brought back to Liskeard for burial and Mary, a widow at 49, and her four children had to consider how they would manage without their breadwinner.

It seems that the family were not left destitute. Donald had died intestate and Letters of Administration were granted to Mary on August 29th 1866 on his personal estate and effects with a value of up to £800. Mary found employment as Mistress of a girls' school in Church Street with a salary of £30 per year and the Mathesons moved to a much larger home at No.1 Pound Street.

By 1881 Mary was making full use of the extra rooms in what was also called Pound House, as she had started her own private day school. Mary at age 64 was the School Mistress and her daughters Rose (32), her Assistant Teacher and Harriet (30), the School Teacher. Son Frank at 22 was living at home and had started a career in banking. Mary died aged 79 in October 1898 having successfully recovered from such a tragic setback in her life.

The snowbound Castle Park with Castle Gardens behind, on April 24th 1908

Pound House where Mrs. Matheson ran her school in 1881

Frank Matheson had progressed to Bank
Accountant by 1911 and was living in the
spacious No.1 Tremeddan Terrace with his
wife, his unmarried sister Rose, two
daughters and two sons, one of whom was
named Donald after the grandfather who
had met with such an untimely death forty-
five years earlier.

FARMING, MINING, PHOTOGRAPHY & DRAPERY
THE COLLIVER FAMILY

Taken from the Bible Christian register of births is:
*'John, the son of John Colliver of the Parish of
Perranarworthal, County of Cornwall, Butcher and of
Elizabeth his wife, who was the daughter of John and Ann
Trebilcock, was born on the 3rd day of June in the year of our
Lord, one thousand eight hundred and twenty seven, and was
solemnly Baptized with water, in the Name of the Father, and
of the Son, and of the Holy Ghost, on the fourth day of
November in the same year of our Lord, at Hicksmill Chapel
in the Parish of Gwennap, County aforesaid, by me Richard
Sedwell, Minister'.*

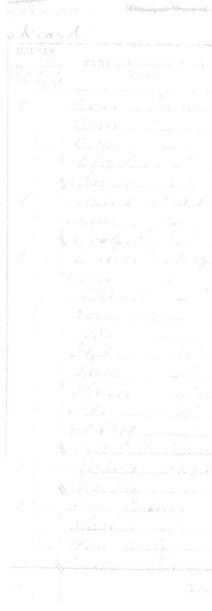

After earlier occupations of Agricultural Labourer at
the age of 14 and Steam Whim Driver in a mine at
25, John Colliver (35, a Photographic Artist)
appeared in the 1861 census for Church Street,
Liskeard. With him were his wife Elizabeth (31,
Milliner) and Elizabeth's sister, Jane Holman (19, also
a Milliner). Previously the Holman sisters were living
in Dobwalls with their father William, whose
occupation was given as *'employed in search for mines'*.

In his booklet *Liskeard Bygones*, Jack Howarth
suggests that Mr. Colliver could have had the first
photography business in Liskeard. The Liskeard &
District Museum booklet *Looking Glass* tells us that
*'By 1858 Mr. Colliver was running his own photographic
business, charging between 6d and £1 to the Nobility, Gentry
and Public Generally'.* John K. Broad in his column in
the *Cornish Times* wrote how Mr.Colliver took a
photograph of him as a baby in a perambulator, in
about 1870, with one foot blurred due to his
constant kicking. The only example of his work
located in Liskeard & District Museum is that of an
unnamed boy posing with a chaise longue. Printed
on the reverse of that photograph is an
advertisement for his services at No.1 Market Street.

John K Broad taken by J.H. Colliver about 1870

Both Howarth and Broad describe the Collivers as rather eccentric and *'dressed in Elizabethan style, he in a tall hat and she in silk bustles'*. It was rumoured that they were left a legacy, but squandered it by *'posing as aristocrats, driving through Liskeard in a low carriage with a pair of greys'*. By the 1901 census, the money had run dry, the photography business had ended and the Collivers were shopkeepers in Barras Street; John a Draper and Elizabeth still a Milliner. John Colliver died the following year and from Broad again *'his wife carried on business as a milliner, but her taste in this direction favouring somewhat of the miraculous'*.

A steam whim, or winding, engine hoisted ore from the depths of a mine. It was powered by a beam engine which was operated by the driver

J.H. Colliver's business card

HEROINES AND HENS

SISTERS DOROTHY AND CECILY PENROSE FOSTER

In the London Gazette supplement dated June 4th 1918 the following citation appeared for the awarding of the Military Medal to Sister Dorothy Penrose Foster, R.R.C., T.F.N.S. *'For conspicuous coolness and devotion to duty when supervising the transfer of patients from a Casualty Clearing Station to an Ambulance Train while the locality of the Casualty Clearing Station was being steadily shelled. She set a splendid example of calmness and composure'.* Dorothy grew up in Coombe House, Lamellion, along with her four sisters and two brothers. Her next home, from 1897 was Trevillis House on Lodge Hill, which later bore a plaque with the following wording *'Dorothy Penrose Foster M.M., R.R.C., T.F.N.S. (1875-1953) lived in this house, which was built by her father Lewis C. Foster'.* When her father died in 1923, Dorothy and 3 of her sisters purchased a plot of land adjoining Trevillis House for £262 10s and built themselves and their mother a new home named Penmilder.

The Military Medal, which was awarded to very few women, together with 5 other medals awarded to Dorothy, were donated to Liskeard & District Museum, but unfortunately, in 2013 they were all stolen and sold by the thief to an unscrupulous dealer for £250. When the theft was reported in the Press some time later a gentleman, who had purchased the medals in good faith for £4,000, returned them to the museum and sued the dealer for the return of his money. They are now kept in the museum safe, protected by a state of the art security system.

Dorothy Penrose Foster's Medals can be viewed by appointment in Liskeard's Museum

Penmilder on Lodge Hill in 1959

Lewis Foster was a founding director of the East Cornwall Bank on the Parade in 1807, it ultimately became part of Barclays Bank

Another heroine in the Foster family was Dorothy's younger sister Cecily Penrose Foster M.B.E. Together with 2 more medals Cecily was awarded the M.B.E. (Military) in recognition of her work with the British Red Cross in France during WWI. Sadly, Cecily met with a fatal accident at only 41 years of age. As well as a love of motoring, Cecily was a keen climber and it was on one of her annual mountaineering holidays that the accident occurred, during an avalanche in the Austrian Tyrol on New Year's Day, 1927.

Perhaps another interest of Cecily's was poultry, as a little while later the following advertisement was placed in the *Cornish Times* '*Mr. Hedley Collings has been instructed to sell by public auction at Penmilder, Liskeard, on Thursday 27th October at 2.30pm, 250 fowls, poultry houses and appliances, the property of Miss D. Foster J.P.'*

65

RUNAWAY WAGONS AND A BOLTING HORSE
RUNNALLS & SONS

On June 7th 1900 the *Cornish Times* reported that *'on Wednesday morning Dairyman Tom Acland of Welltown was delivering milk in Dean Street when his horse bolted towards the Post Office. Builder Richard Runnalls, of Victoria Terrace, Station Road and one of his workmen, who were passing at the time with a ladder, held it across the street for the purpose of stopping it. The horse however leapt over the ladder, overturning the trio and throwing the milk cans, and a quantity of eggs into the street. The horse then proceeded down Bay Tree Hill and on to Tanyard Hill where a wheel of the trap caught in a telegraph pole, and the horse was stopped. It was very plucky of Mr. Runnalls to attempt to stop the horse; the ladder was broken and Mr. Runnalls slightly injured'.*

Possibly one of the most challenging contracts for Runnalls & Sons of No.1 Victoria Terrace was the building of the Prince of Wales engine house at Phoenix United Mine on Bodmin Moor. In 1907 a regular correspondence took place between Richard Runnalls and Horace Holbrook, Superintendent of the Liskeard & Caradon Railway, whose branch line was used by Runnalls to deliver materials to their building site. It concerned the regular damage to the L&CR wagons by the Runnalls' workforce. On June 11th Holbrook wrote *'I note a wagon is smashed, this is unfortunate and ought not to have happened. You do not say whether it is still in the mine shaft, but it must not be used again until I have seen it'.* On July 3rd Holbrook received a report that *'Mr. Runnalls' men at the Phoenix Branch have again let two wagons run away down the main road into the mine, knocking the buffer and front wheels off one wagon, and the wheels off the other'.*

Despite this unfortunate episode Runnalls & Sons built many important buildings in Liskeard, including Pencubitt House, the Post Office in Windsor Place, Victoria, Bonython and Rosemellon Terraces and Dobwalls Memorial Hall. Richard himself became Chairman of the Liskeard Master Builders Association for many years. At his funeral on June 15th 1930 his six oldest employees carried his coffin from his home

across the street to Lanchard Cemetery. Meanwhile a numerous Civic Procession left the Guildhall headed by the Mayor, two Aldermen, nine Councillors and the Sergeants at Mace, a sign of the respect in which he was held by his fellow townspeople.

The Old Post Office on the corner of Bay Tree Hill and Windsor Place

The Prince of Wales engine house during construction in 1907

'Possibly one of the most challenging contracts for Runnalls & Sons of No.1 Victoria Terrace was the building of the Prince of Wales engine house at Phoenix United Mine on Bodmin Moor.'

WATERCOLOURS AND KNIT FROCKS
BROAD FAMILY

1844 is the first year that Joseph Broad, at the age of 50 appeared in *Kelly's Trade Directory* as a *Grocer at 27 Church Street, Liskeard*. In August 1855 Joseph attended a public auction at Webb's Hotel to bid for the *'dwelling house, shop, courtledge and garden'* that he had been leasing for 10s per year from the Kekewich Estate. His bid of £210 was successful and Broad's Store was now firmly established, specialising in quality groceries such as Goundry's Patent Consolidated Teas, who advertised *"a new era for tea drinkers"*.

After Joseph's death in 1865 his son John and daughter-in-law Sarah took over the business. Their six children were born above the store, they included John Kerkin Broad in 1869 and Richard Kerkin Broad in 1875.

From an early age John assisted his parents, and later his younger brother Arthur, in the running of the family business, but he was a man of many other talents. He trained with Stanhope and Elizabeth Forbes in their Newlyn School of Art and become a member of the British Watercolour Society, which enabled him to use the letters BWS after his name. In the 1920s and 30s his paintings were popular in Liskeard as wedding presents. John also took an interest in china and pottery and was an early stockist of Clarice Cliff products. On the *Antiques Roadshow* in 2021 a Cliff vase was valued at £2000 and a plate from her Sunburst range at £10,000! John had a deep interest in local history and in the 1930s wrote a regular column in the *Cornish Times* entitled *'While I Remember'*, which gave a valuable insight into everyday life in 19th century Liskeard.

Richard K Broad outside his Fore Street tailor shop

Caroline or Sarah Broad outside the family store in Church Street in 1899

Richard had a successful tailor shop at 11 Fore Street, Liskeard, named Yarmouth Stores and when he moved to larger premises at no.16, his sign simply said Broad. Another side to Richard's business was purchasing quantities of five ply yarn from Tippett & Sons in Plymouth. He then travelled on a regular basis to Polperro where he sold the yarn to the fishwives, who would knit the traditional Polperro Knit Frock, or gansey, for their husbands. There were always more Knit Frocks than was required in Polperro and these Richard

purchased and then sent to Yarmouth where he had contacts to purchase them, hence the name of his first shop. His early trips to Polperro were by motor cycle and side-car, but he met with an accident in which he lost the tips of several fingers. After that he bought an old Brooke Bond Tea van and employed a man to drive him. Richard also supplied the Union Workhouse in Station Road with grey pinstripe frocks with white aprons for females and brown corduroy or serge suits for the males.

THACKERAY AND DICKENS
FAMOUS VISITORS TO LISKEARD

From a collection of letters written by William Makepeace Thackeray, the following is dated June 21st 1832 *'When we crossed the water to Torpoint and set off to Liskeard by the mail our first act was a blunder. We went to the wrong inn. This however was soon remedied, our trunks were withdrawn and ourselves. Breakfasted at Mr. Lyne's the Attorney, a shrewd sensible snob of a fellow'.*

The *'wrong inn'* was The Bell in Church Street which was the subject of a disturbing report in *The West Briton* newspaper in September 1858, *'There was considerable excitement in Liskeard over the death of Daniel Dunnaway, a miner at Wheal Trehane, from the effects of a wound in the abdomen in a street fight with William Ball, a miner of St. Cleer, on Saturday night. Both had spent the evening at the Bell Tap and left together walking up Church Street. There was a fight and Ball stabbed Donnaway who walked home, with help, to Pengover Green where he died. Ball was later sentenced to 4 years imprisonment for manslaughter'.*

The East Cornwall Hunt outside the Old Stag in the 1940s or 1950s

The Red Lion in Lower Lux Street in the 1940s or 1950s

Thackeray's *'trunks were withdrawn'* to The Red Lion in Lower Lux Street which is thought to be one of the oldest inns in Liskeard. Appearing before the Borough Magistrates in 1670, the landlord was accused of *'keeping a shuffle board and other unlawful games and for running a bad house'*. The *'shrewd sensible snob of a fellow'* was Benjamin Hart-Lyne the election agent for Charles Buller, who Thackeray was in Liskeard to support during the election of 1832. The scene of their breakfast was Wadham House, Hart-Lyne's mansion in Church Street South which is now apartments.

Another 19th century visitor to Liskeard was Charles Dickens who wrote to his sister-in-law Georgina Hogarth from Bideford in Devon on November 1st 1860. *'I write, with the most impracticable iron pen on earth, to report our safe arrival here, in a beastly hotel. We start tomorrow morning at nine on a two days' posting between this and Liskeard in Cornwall. We are due in Liskeard on Saturday afternoon and we purpose making an excursion in that neighbourhood on Sunday, coming up from Liskeard on Monday by Great Western fast train which will get us to London, please God, in good time on Monday evening.'*

It is not known in which hostelry Dickens spent the nights of Saturday and Sunday, November 3rd and 4th, but the newly built Stag Hotel would have been the most convenient for the railway station. We do know that he was not very impressed with his hotel in Bideford, *'We had stinking fish for dinner and have been able to drink nothing, although we have ordered wine, beer and brandy with water. There is nothing in the house but two tarts and a pair of snuffers. The landlady is playing cribbage in the next room, behind a thin partition, and they seem quite comfortable!'*

A TIPSY ENGRAVER?

PETER HITT

On the first floor of the Royal Cornwall Museum in Truro is a longcase clock with the following information, *'Pine-cased two train cottage clock with 30 hour bird cage movement made by Peter Hitt of Liskeard (1748-1803); cleaned and restored by A.R. Williams of Plymouth Clock Centre'*. At the Truro Auction Centre on March 15th 2013 was the following lot: *'An 18th century Cornish long case clock by Peter Hitt of Liskeard with 10 inch brass square dial and 8 day movement in later mahogany traditional style case'*.

Initially Peter Hitt learnt the trade of Gunsmith from his father, also Peter Hitt. The latter paid the duty on his Apprentice's Indenture on September 24th 1762. The apprentice was Nathaniel Harris who would be instructed in the art of Gunsmith. Whereas Peter Hitt junior on May 29th 1782 paid the duty for his apprentice, Thomas Austin and instructed him in the art of Clockmaker.

Peter Hitt appears twice in the Mayor of Liskeard's accounts, in 1777 for cleaning the Town Hall clock and in 1784 for repairing it

From the June 2000 issue of the Clock Magazine

A 30-hour dark stained pine longcase clock by Peter Hitt of Liskeard was featured in the June 2000 issue of the periodical *Clocks*. The three page article includes the following: *'The maker Peter Hitt has his name engraved on an arched piece of brass, attached to the dial above the six o'clock position, P.Hitt Liskeard. Evidently the person doing this engraving wasn't a skilled or well-practised engraver (or maybe he had too many glasses of beer with his lunch?). If you follow the engraving around starting with the maker's name, it becomes apparent that the spacing between the letters becomes progressively smaller. Now, by the time the engraver got to the town name he knew that there might be a problem! However, he bravely carried on, it is only when he got to the K of Liskeard that he knew things weren't going to plan. If you look at the photograph of the dial, note that the last letter D of Liskeard sits as a small neat addition above this word'.*

Clock Magazine Front cover

Peter Hitt is named in a lease held at Kresen Kernow dated 1802, whereby he would rent a house and garden in Church Street South from Mary Connock of Treworgey Manor for 6 shillings annual rent. The document is marked 'Uncompleted' as Peter Hitt died before he had added his signature. As he had died intestate his wife Mary had to apply for Letters of Administration which were not granted until October 7th 1803. Mary, together with a Cordwainer named John Smithy and Yeoman Thomas Coppin had to sign a bond for £200, to be paid if a Will with a different beneficiary turned up within one year. Coppin was the only one of the three who could sign his name, Mary's mark was 'O' and Smithy's was 'X'.

Bodgara Mill photographed in the 1950s

A GRATUITOUS ADVOCATE
WILLIAM RAWLE AND THE BULL STONE RIOT

On January 2nd 1792 Richard Rawle, Gentleman of Liskeard, signed Articles of Clerkship which bound his son William to serve Peter Goodman Glubb, Attorney of Liskeard, as his Clerk for the term of five years, when William would became 21 years old.

John Allen, writing in 1856, informs us that a large stone, furnished with an iron ring for bull baiting, was formerly fixed in the centre of the Bull Post (now The Parade). About 1792 it was moved to the lower part of Barrel (now Barras) Street and used by one of the Aldermen as a horse block. Many of the towns people drew the stone back to the Bull Post. This was regarded by the irate authorities as a direct insult offered to themselves. The Riot Act was read, the chief parties, including W. Rawle Esq., were committed to the King's Bench Court and in a compromise, the Bull Stone was removed to the Market House, and eventually to Castle Park where it is today. At Kresen Kernow in Redruth are stored documents described as *'Brief for the prosecution, case, indictment, examination of witnesses etc. in Rex versus William Rawle and others at Bodmin Assizes, King's Bench 1802'*. This action was taken as a consequence of the Bull Stone Riot.

Also from John Allen is an offer by William Rawle to give his services free of charge: *The Corporation compelled the inhabitants to grind all their corn there (at Bodgara Mill), but an individual, in defiance of this authority, and sending his grist to some other mill, a suit of law was instituted against him, when he and other inhabitants found a gratuitous advocate in W. Rawle Esq., solicitor of the town, and were successful in freeing themselves from the obligation. The consequence was that a large part of the custom was withdrawn'.* In 1487 the fine for grinding corn at other than the Town Mill was 6d. This had risen to 3s 4d by 1669 when 9 townspeople were fined.

William Rawle became a man of means in Liskeard, appearing in connection with 4 separate properties in the Land Tax Assessment of 1798. He married Elizabeth Garland in July 1803 and they are both interred in a grand Grade II listed chest tomb in St. Martin's churchyard.

There are five Grade II listed tombs in St. Martin's Churchyard: Knight the Publican, Fitze the Tanner, Lyne of Wadham, Glencross of Luxstowe and Rawle the Attorney

The Bull Stone in Castle Park, Castle Street

THE WEDDING OF MAUD HOBHOUSE

On August 31st 1889 the *Cornish Times* reported on *'the occasion of the wedding of Miss Maud Hobhouse, parishioners assembled in large numbers in St. Ive churchyard and a flag was flown from the tower'.* Maud was born and grew up in The Rectory, St. Ive, she was 30 when she married the Rev. E. Presgrave Hebblethwaite, vicar of Poundstock, near Bude. Maud was the second eldest daughter of the Ven. Archdeacon Reginald Hobhouse, rector of St. Ive. The census of 1871 lists the Hobhouse family as Reginald (53), wife Caroline (50), daughters Blanche (13), Maud (12) and Emily (10) and son Leonard (6). To look after them was a Governess and five, yes five, domestic servants.

'The bride's dress, of white brocaded silk with a Brussels lace front and a Court train, as well as those of the bridesmaids, were made by the Misses B. and E. Thomas of Fore Street, Liskeard'. In 1891 sisters Bessie (46) and Ellen (23) Thomas were in business as Dressmakers. Also in the census for that year were another sister, Mary Andrews, a widowed Housekeeper, Mary's son Harry, who at 16 was employed in the business, and Maud Richards, a Dressmaker aged 14.

'After breakfast at The Rectory, Mr. & Mrs. Hepplethwaite drove to Liskeard, taking the 1.30pm train to Plymouth' en route to their honeymoon at Spye Park, Wiltshire, courtesy of the owner Captain Spicer. Now known as The Chantry, the former Rectory in St. Ive is now owned by the Emily Estate (UK) and is being restored to become a museum dedicated to the life and work of the civil rights campaigner Emily Hobhouse, who is still revered in South Africa.

Maud Hobhouse on the right, with her sister Emily

For the interment of Emily Hobhouse's ashes at the Women's Memorial, shops and businesses were closed all day in Bloemfontein and flags were at half-mast

The Rectory, St. Ive now called The Chantry

Among the bridesmaids was Miss Emily Hobhouse, sister of the bride. On July 7th 1900 the *Cornish Times* reported that *"a public meeting was held at the Public Hall, Liskeard, on Thursday evening, under the auspices of the South Africa Conciliation Committee, in order to advocate an early close to the conflict with the Boers. Mr. A.T. Quiller Couch, of Fowey, the well-known novelist, presided, and the speakers were announced to be Miss Ellen Robinson of Liverpool, Miss Emily Hobhouse, secretary of the Conciliation Committee, and Mr. Lloyd George, the Radical member for Carnarvon."* The headlines were 'Uproarious Proceedings', 'Speakers Refused a Hearing', 'Platform Stormed' and 'Meeting Broke up in Disorder'. Not Liskeard's finest hour in history!

Having been a member for seventeen years, the St. Ive Church Choir presented Maud with *'a beautiful silver mounted china biscuitiere'*, which was supplied by Messrs. Botterell & Son of Fore Street, Liskeard. Maud had been an Associate of the Girls Friendly Society for ten years and they *'united in presenting a very handsome bronze duplex lamp'*.

LIVING IN FILTH AND FOUL AIR

On the Historic England record of listed buildings are an *'early/mid-19th century pair of small houses and attached coach house'* in Westbourne Lane. The houses were originally built to accommodate the overwhelming influx of miners from West Cornwall to seek employment in the newly opened copper mines around Caradon Hill. The coach house was also small houses and the area was named Bowden's Court after the owner John Bowden who, in the census of 1851, was the oldest man in Liskeard at 91. He was a widowed Land Proprietor (formerly a Wool Carder) and living in nearby Dean Street with his 28 year old Domestic Servant Mary Dyer.

Wheal Honey & Trelawny United, the last remains of lead mining in Menheniot

Westbourne Lane, previously Bowden's Court, in 2017

Local architect Henry Rice reported regularly to the Town Council on the unsanitary nature of the overcrowded Courts in Liskeard which led to his appointment as Inspector of Nuisances. In 1865 he submitted a reported entitled Mr. Bowden's Premises in the Lane behind Dean Street, this Mr. Bowden being John's son William. The report was damning, *'The Courtlage is a filthy disgusting place and requires immediate and thorough cleansing and draining. The old cottages abutting on this Courtlage are wretched hovels especially those facing the lane which have dung piled against the back wall of the Court, soaking through the same into the living rooms rendering the place indecent and unwholesome. In these cottages there are fifty three persons without a vestage of privy accommodation, consequently they live in the middle of filth and foul air and the wonder is that they live at all!'*

So who were the unfortunate fifty three persons living, as Rice claimed, in conditions with a high risk of contracting cholera? The disease had claimed twenty seven lives in Liskeard in 1832 and another fifteen in 1849. The fifty three residents in 1861 are too many names to list here, but a high proportion of these were children, many of whom returned to these awful conditions after a long day's work in the mines. These examples from Bowden's Court are typical of the times: James Esterbrook (17, Copper Miner), William Wills (17, Roper), John Lander (16, Lead Miner), William Burrell (15, Lead Miner), John Harris (14, Lead Miner) and his brother William Harris (13, Lead Miner). When you also consider that the nearest lead mines were a three mile walk away in Menheniot, it is little wonder that these children could not expect to live beyond the average life expectancy for a miner of forty, that's if they did not meet with one of the mining accidents that were commonplace at the time.

FIRE! FIRE! FIRE!

The original 1841 Wesley Chapel in Barn Street, by local architect Henry Rice, was much smaller than the present one. Tragically on June 6th 1845 it was burned down by arsonists. The intense heat was such that glass in windows across the street were shattered. Over 200 people fought the flames, but after about an hour the roof fell in. The Chapel was uninsured! Yet such was the devotion and self-sacrifice of the congregation that they immediately set about the task of raising money to build a new and larger one, at the forefront of this effort were two boys, Henry Lucas and Andrew Hingston.

The boys resolved that *'we will give all we can, and beg all we can, to build a Chapel, and that we will begin at once'*, their subscription list started with their own savings; Henry £20 and Andrew £18. Within four months, on September 23rd 1845 the foundation stone for the present building was laid. Henry later became an Ironmonger in Fore Street and Andrew a Surgeon in Dean Street.

The Wesley Chapel, now named the Methodist Church, in Barn Street, 1910

The *Cornish Times* headlines on September 7th 1923 were 'The Fatal Fire at Liskeard, Thrilling Accounts of the Double Tragedy and Bravery of the Firemen and Constable'. The fire resulted in the loss of two lives and the destruction of a terrace containing two cottages, the office of Auctioneer James H. Daw and several tenanted rooms above. Currently unoccupied, the site was until recently the ATS Tyre Depot in Dean Street.

Mr. Thomas Cornish, a Journeyman Baker aged 63, was assisting an upstairs tenant in the saving of her belongings by carrying drawers from a dresser down an unlit staircase. Mr. Cornish tripped and fell, striking his head on a low beam and he died soon after from a fracture to the skull. When a fireman entered an upstairs bedroom he found it full of dense smoke and 73 year old Miss Jane Stephens lying unconscious on the floor. He lifted her up and passed her through an open window to a colleague who was waiting on a fire ladder. Artificial respiration was applied but to no avail; Dr. Garrard from the nearby Rosedean Surgery told the inquest that *'the woman was very deaf and if anyone had hammered on her door for a month she would never had heard them'*.

A Peek into Liskeard's Past

On August 23rd 1935 the Cornish Times reported that *'within four years of reaching the centenary of its erection the Temperance Hall in Barn Street, on Saturday was threatened with destruction by fire. Only effective measures by the Fire Brigade quelled a dangerous outbreak after considerable damage had been done to the building and its contents'*. For only a week the occupants had been Lockyer & Wolff, dealers in bankrupt and salvage stock, and the hall's platform was filled with drapery, rugs and fancy goods, amongst which the fire started.

When smoke was seen by neighbour Mr. Richard Toms of the Windsor Dairy, he ran to the Market House and rang the electric fire alarm. Within minutes the Fire Brigade arrived and when the front doors of the hall were opened *'the scene within revealed the alarming nature of the fire. From end to end the platform was ablaze, the inflammable drapery goods sending up orange and crimson flames 5ft or 6ft in height, whilst billowing smoke clouds filled the building'*. The trustees decided to sell the hall which passed through several hands with many alterations until the current occupants, the Royal British Legion club moved in 1978.

Before moving to Greenbank Road the Fire Station was at the top of Fairpark Road, in the building that then became home to the St John Ambulance service

The fire in Dean Street in the early hours of Tuesday September 4th 1923

SMUGGLERS AND AN OVERBLOWN ROSE
THE CORNER OF FORE STREET AND BAY TREE HILL

Up to the 1830s the town house of John Connock, owner of the Manor of Treworgey and a Mayor of Liskeard, was on the corner of Bay Tree Hill and Fore Street, where M. & Co. is today. The building became the notorious Talbot Inn; in 1869 prostitute Tilly Cowling stole 10s from a St. Juliot Farmer and R. Abraham assaulted the landlady for refusing him further drinks. Both offences took place in the Talbot and both offenders were fined by the Magistrates.

The landlord of the Talbot for many years was Thomas Coath, whose main source of income, it was rumoured, was not from the liquor he sold legally, but from what he bought, namely a little contraband. The proof of this was a discovery in later years under an exceptionally large window seat in one of the bedchambers. Embedded deep in the masonry and secured with mortar were two large stone jars capable of holding around six gallons of smuggled spirits. To avoid detection by the Revenue Officers two beautiful flower pots, one containing a geranium and the other a myrtle, were placed on the window seat. Beneath each pot was a neatly disguised hole, just large enough to hold a funnel to pour liquor into, or draw it out, of the hidden jars. The smugglers in those days came mainly from Cawsand and Talland with their contraband goods, it was said that they stopped in Liskeard en-route to the infamous Jamaica Inn.

By the time of the 1871 census Mary and Elizabeth Stantan occupied the now former Talbot Inn, which they had converted to house their retail premises. The Stantan sisters gave employment to twelve women, two girls and three boys. Their 1871 trade directory entry was *'linen & wool draper, milliner, hosier, haberdasher, hats, caps & mourning outfitter'*. The staff living above the store with the Stantans were a Dressmaker, two Shop Assistants and a Domestic Servant.

Cornish Times columnist J.K. Broad recalled the Stantans, *'there were two sisters, both keen business women, but it was Miss Mary I remember best. Like a large kind overblown rose, she had a reputation for being a very fine dancer, but of huge proportions. It was surely fortunate that she could trip the fantastic lightly or someone would be the worse for wear'*.

November 14th 1968 is still remembered by many as the day that fire ripped through the Victorian building at the end of Fore Street, at that time the premises of another successful clothing store, Maggs, Son & Deeble. Above the store were apartments, one was occupied by a newly married couple who lost all their possessions in the fire. An appeal to help them was made and enough was collected in the town to replace all that they had lost. Nearby shops were closed during the fire and the staff of F.W. Woolworth & Co., immediately opposite, remained at work making tea and sandwiches for the Firemen working to stop the blaze spreading further.

On the left is the Stantan & Stantan store in Fore Street in 1906

The fire at Maggs, Son & Deeble in Fore Street on November 14th 1968

SAD DAYS IN TREMAR AND LISKEARD

PETER CLYMO

Grade II listed Dean House in Dean Street was built by Henry Rice in 1855 for Peter and Mary Clymo. In 1861 they employed Amelia Blamey (27) as Cook and Charlotte Bowden (21) as Housemaid. Now called Graylands it houses the Register Office with what is thought to be the last remaining WWII bunker in Liskeard under the front lawn. On December 14th 1872 the *Cornish Times* reported on The Great Storm, *'at Mrs. Clymo's house in Dean Street a kitchen chimney was blown down and fell through the roof to the kitchen below, the residents were absent at the time'.* The former Clymos' drawing room with its lovely bay windows and view of the garden is now the Marriage Room.

With his brother James, Peter Clymo discovered copper on the slopes of Caradon Hill in 1836. The area became South Caradon Mine which, by 1873 employed six hundred people and had the highest copper output of any mine in Cornwall. Among several other mining interests, he was also Manager and Purser at Wheal Mary Ann lead/silver mine in Menheniot where over four hundred were employed. The workforce there presented a fine silver-plate tray to him, which is on display in Liskeard & District Museum, *'as a testimonial of their respect and esteem'.*

South Caradon Mine prior to its closure in 1885

Graylands in Dean Street with its Bunker under the front lawn

Having worked underground himself, Peter Clymo was concerned for the welfare of his workers. He provided a heated building for the drying and changing of clothes, a man-engine was installed to dispense with the scaling of many fathoms of ladders before and after each shift, and he supported the establishment of the Caradon Miners' & Mechanics' Friendly Society. Not all mining accidents could be avoided though, the *West Briton* reported on December 1st 1870 that *'a number of men were engaged in putting in a flywheel at South Caradon Mine on Saturday. John Oliver of Tremar Coombe slipped and his foot was caught in the wheel. Both his legs were broken and he died just before arriving home, he left a wife and 8 children'.*

Peter Clymo died on July 28th 1870 and on the day of his funeral, shops in Liskeard were shuttered and normal business ceased for the day. The cortege was led through the town by his family and friends followed by the Mayor, Aldermen and Councillors, then came eleven hundred miners with a further one thousand towns-people lining the streets.

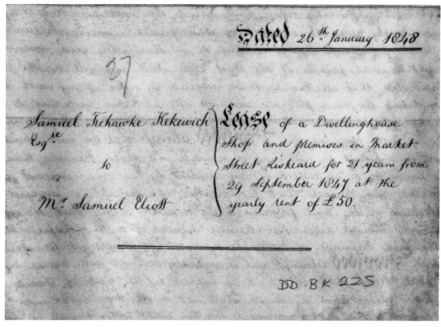

Samuel Eliott's Lease dated January 26th 1848

CHEESE AND LEECHES

No.6 MARKET STREET

On January 26th 1848 Mr. Samuel Eliott signed a twenty one year lease for *'a Dwelling house, Shop and premises in Market Street, Liskeard at the yearly rent of £50'*. His landlord was Samuel Trehawke Kekewich Esq., who seven years later sold the freehold to Eliott for £970. The property in question was No.6 Market Street, which at present is occupied by the Fat Frog Café.

A series of sketches of many of the smaller English boroughs appeared in the *Daily News* in 1848, it was the turn of Liskeard on December 18th. *'We take the best looking shop in town, a shop of some pretension, in the best street, with a plate glass front, and some slight ornament and style about it. The proprietor is apparently a chemist and, as you will find by a certificate suspended in his window, a member of the Pharmaceutical Society. Well, you enter and you find his trade is by no means confined to the sale of chemicals and drugs. Your nose is not overpowered, as it is in some places, by the smell of rhubarb. Here there is a mingled perfume of sweetness. You find that you may purchase here many other things besides syrup of squills. There are things to make you ill, as well as to cure you. The bane is sold as well as the antidote. Here you may have bacon and ipecacuanha, fresh butter and pitch plasters, the best London pickles and Holloway's ointment, Wiltshire cheese and leeches, in fact, the pick of an excellent general assortment'.* The shop described was Eliott's in Market Street.

In May 1857 Samuel Eliott, Grocer & Chemist, announced that he had recently been appointed Manager of the Plymouth Soap Co. and was leaving Liskeard. A tea was held in his honour at the Temperance Hall by the Liskeard Teetotal Society of which he was a member, one hundred and eighty attended and a silver teapot with a value of £15.00, was presented to him.

The 1861 census tells us that Whinfield and Caroline Robinson were in business at No.6 Market Street employing eight men and four boys, with a warehouse in nearby Well Lane. In 1871 Whinfield was elected to the Town Council with the highest number of votes of all the candidates. As a member of the Temperance Society he supported the Licensing Act which would lower the closing time of public houses from 1.00am to 11.00pm, and to 10.00pm on Sundays. Family life was tragic for the Robinsons; four of their children died under the age of 1 year and another died at age 6, all are buried in the Halbathick Quaker cemetery at Trevecca, Liskeard, where several members of the Eliott family, being Quakers as well as the Robinsons, are also buried.

In 2021 the current owners, during exterior redecoration, uncovered the beautiful signage of the Home & Colonial store, occupiers of the premises for many years in the previous century.

In the 1870s Mary Stallard, 65 year old widowed cook at Tremeddan House (as per pages 36–37) was a customer of Eliott's, her purchases, apart from groats and blacking, were similar to those of today.

The signage of a previous occupier uncovered in 2021

index
Page numbers in *italics* indicate illustrations